U.S. MARINE COMBAT CONDITIONING

U.S. MARINE COMBAT CONDITIONING

United States Marine Corps

Introduction by Jack Hoban, Subject Matter Expert,
Marine Corps Martial Arts Program

Skyhorse Publishing

Skyhorse Publishing books may be purchased in bulk at special discounts for
sales promotion, corporate gifts, fund-raising, or educational purposes. Special
editions can also be created to specifications. For details, contact the Special Sales
Department, Skyhorse Publishing, 307 West 36th Street, 11th Floor, New York,
NY 10018 or info@skyhorsepublishing.com.

www.skyhorsepublishing.com

10 9 8 7 6 5 4 3 2 1

Library of Congress Cataloging-in-Publication Data

U.S. Marine combat conditioning / United States Marine Corps.
    p. cm.
  ISBN 978-1-60239-962-4 (pbk. : alk. paper)
  1. United States. Marine Corps--Handbooks, manuals, etc. 2. United States.
Marine Corps--Physical training--Handbooks, manuals, etc. 3. Soldiers--Training
of--United States. 4. Combat--Handbooks, manuals, etc. 5. Hand-to-hand
fighting--Handbooks, manuals, etc. I. United States. Marine Corps.
  VE153.U17 2011
  359.96'4--dc22
                              2010040523

Printed in China

INTRODUCTION

In this day of counterinsurgencies and "small wars," it is extremely enlightening to review this Combat Conditioning Program manual, which was originally published less than a year before the end of World War II. The United States had been in a full-scale war for nearly three years, and the seriousness and scope of this manual reflects the atmosphere of "total war" as well as the lessons learned—and eventually unlearned or forgotten—with a bloody bayonet in hand.

I recall seeing several Marine Corps Close Combat training films from the 1940s. One was a clip from a bayonet fighting training film from before the war, while another was a close combat training film made near the end of the war. What a contrast! The first clip showed an almost humorous "ballet" of grown men moving like robots, gingerly poking the air with their bayonets. The latter, on the other hand, was very serious business. You could easily tell that the second film was created by men who had actually used these techniques in combat. The tone of that second film is consistent with the book you hold in your hand—grim and realistic.

The first portion of the program contains unglamorous but sensible techniques clearly designed to build flexibility, strength, and endurance for the close-in fight. The manual's conditioning regimen includes solo training, paired training, and group training. Next, the manual covers a rather exhaustive set of unarmed and armed "dirty" fighting techniques. There are also many techniques that appear to be "police" techniques, perhaps due to the influence of William E. "Dan" Fairbain (1885–1960), a British close combat expert and policeman who trained Marines in China and elsewhere. Although Fairbain's forte was knife-fighting—and he is usually known for that—he was also a policeman in Shanghai for many years. He may have been the source of the "come alongs" included in the manual, which were clearly designed for managing prisoners.

The other interesting thing about this manual is the title. You may have noticed that the name of the book is *Combat Conditioning* while most of the book is devoted to hand-to-hand close combat. This lack of a distinction between conditioning and fighting techniques should be noted. Clearly, close combat can be very physically exhausting.

A manual that covers both the actual close combat techniques as well as the conditioning regimen necessary to perform those techniques—particularly if the Marine is sleep-, food-, and water-deprived—makes perfect sense. Yet, the two disciplines were softened and separated later during the Cold War.

When I was a Marine in the 1970s and 1980s, we ran the obstacle course and participated in conditioning hikes, but our "combat stamina" was measured and scored by the Physical Fitness Test (PFT). The PFT consisted of sit-ups, pull-ups, and a three-mile run. Rather than combat utility uniforms and boots (not to mention helmets and flak jackets and gear), we wore running shorts, T-shirts, and sneakers—ostensibly to avoid heel and shin injuries. Ridiculous? You bet.

The fact that the various armed services (it wasn't just the Marine Corps) seemed to forget the lessons of World War II and the importance of conditioning as a proper preparation for real combat may come as a surprise. But as the pre-WWII films indicated, it wasn't the first time. As far as the actual close combat skills are concerned, there is no way that our Marines and soldiers survived WWI trenches and Belleau Wood using the techniques I saw in that first film.

With the Marine Corps Martial Arts Program (2000) and the Combat Fitness Test (2008), the Marines have started to recover the Close Combat and Combat Conditioning skills Marines need to for contemporary combat. MCMAP is a synergistic combatives program consisting of martial arts, combat mindset training, and ethics. The Combat Fitness Test requires Marines in the utility uniform and combat boots to sprint a timed 880 yards, lift a 30-pound ammunition can overhead from shoulder height repeatedly for two minutes, and perform a maneuver-under-fire event, which is a timed 300-yard shuttle run in which Marines are paired up by size and perform a series of combat-related tasks. Now that's a test of physical readiness!

However, it all prompts the question of why the two disciplines are not combined into one coordinated training program—just as we see it here in *U.S. Marine Combat Conditioning*. That is a mystery, but I suspect that the reason has more to do with a bureaucratic desire to maintain separate fiefdoms as it does to serve the needs of the Marine Corps. It could be argued that the most effective training for close-in fighting would include combat conditioning, martial arts, close-in shooting, psychological training, and ethics in one combined approach. Perhaps that day will come. In the meantime, despite all of the advances that have been made in the separate disciplines—for example, there is no question that we know more about conditioning today than we did in 1943—this manual still has value. It is a reminder that conditioning and combat training go hand in hand.

—Jack Hoban
Subject Matter Expert, Marine Corps Martial Arts Program
President, Resolution Group International

FOREWORD

The purposes of this course in Combat Conditioning are two: first, to maintain the physical condition of Officer Candidates, and while so doing, to teach them the essentials of combat conditioning so that they will later be able to plan and carry out an effective conditioning program; and second, to serve as a guide for units of the Marine Corps in establishment of their own combat conditioning programs.

We realize that the requirements of Combat Conditioning for the various Marine Corps units will differ. For example, weapons units need less bayonet work than infantry units but should have more work in which they hike and exercise with some of their heavy equipment and weapons such as machine guns, mortars, loaded ammunition chests, and the like. While the material in this pamphlet is primarily for the use of rifle units in training, much of it can be used as a guide for a combat conditioning program by any type of Marine unit regardless of size.

This course includes the conducts and movements of mass physical drill and body strengthening exercises; the organization and conduct of competitive games; orientation in and application of the principles and movements of hand-to-hand combat and of disarming and the outline of a comprehensive and effective system of aggressive bayonet fighting. Throughout are stressed those basic techniques and movements most readily learned by Marines in training and which will be most reliable and effective in actual combat.

One important phase of the training of Marines, Combat Swimming and Flotation, has been omitted from this course. The importance of this training is appreciated. The U.S. Navy Bureau of Navy Personnel has produced some excellent publications on the subject of swimming which are available and can be referred to if the necessity arises.

TABLE OF CONTENTS

SECTION 1

COMBAT CONDITIONING

SECTION 2

MASS PHYSICAL DRILL

SECTION 3

JUDO

SECTION 4

PISTOL, SILENT WEAPONS, AND CLUB

SECTION 5

COMPETITIVE GAMES AND EXERCISES

SECTION 6

KNIFE

SECTION 7

BAYONET

iii

TABLE OF ILLUSTRATIONS

Title	Figure	Page

Title	Figure	Page

OFFICER CANDIDATES SCHOOL
MARINE CORPS SCHOOLS
MARINE BARRACKS, QUANTICO, VIRGINIA

COMBAT CONDITIONING PROGRAM

SCOPE: The essentials of physical drill, hand-to-hand combat, disarming, and knife and bayonet fighting; the conduct of combat conditioning programs.

TYPE OF INSTRUCTION: Explanation and demonstration by instructor. Practice by the individual Marine (pairs of men) and by squads or platoons. Close supervision and assistance by company officers and noncommissioned officers.

PLACE: Field.

TOTAL HOURS: Eighteen (18).

LENGTH OF PERIODS: Two consecutive sessions of fifty minutes each.

EQUIPMENT: Clubs, dummy pistols, sawdust pit, surveyed M1903 rifles, cut-down M1903 bayonet scabbards, M1 bayonets, obstacle, bayonet, and combat conditioning courses. (For details see pages 3 and 4).

STUDY REFERENCES: Bayonet, FM 23-25, War Department, Basic Field Manual, 7Sep43.

Combat Conditioning, Marine Corps Schools, Sep44.

Landing Force Manual, United States Navy, 1938.

Physical Fitness Manual for the Navy, Bureau of Naval Personnel, 1943.

Physical Training, FM 21-20, War Department, 6Mar41.

Unarmed Defense for the American Soldier, FM 21-150, 30Jun42.

VISUAL AIDS: None scheduled. However, occasionally inclement weather precluded outdoor instruction and indoor classes were held at which some of the below selection of available training films would be shown.

The three (3) training films listed below are highly recommended as a supplement to any combat conditioning program. They require little or no explanation or correction:

MTF #12 Combat Conditioning; Part I, Accelerated Calisthenics and Elemental Contacts;

MTF #13 Combat Conditioning, Part II, Bayonet Fighting;

MTF #17, Combat Conditioning, Combat Swimming.

The two (2) training films listed below are recommended also but will require a few minor corrections or amplification:

MTF #14 Combat Conditioning, Club and Knife Fighting;

MTF #15 Combat Conditioning, Unarmed Combat.

SECTION 1

COMBAT CONDITIONING

(An introductory lecture given to the Candidates by the Chief, Combat Conditioning Section).

1. Definition.—Combat Conditioning is the physical and mental conditioning of the individual Marine for hand-to-hand combat. It involves toughening him physically by mass physical drill, by hand-to-hand and bayonet fighting, by competitive games, and by frequent runs through specially designed obstacle and assault courses. It develops in him the realization that skill in hand-to-hand combat and bayonet fighting is vital battle equipment. The goal of combat conditioning is not only to develop physical strength, agility, and endurance in every officer and man of the unit undergoing the training, but also to develop in him confidence in himself as a fighting man with the bayonet, the knife, the club, or with no weapons at all.

2. Program, General.—a. Combat Conditioning is an essential part of the progressive training of all Marines. The Combat Conditioning program must be progressive in nature. In addition to conditioning the men physically, the program must be designed to help the men, from the very start, overcome inhibitions for physical contact. It must develop in them eagerness to close with the enemy and confidence in each man in his own and in his comrades' abilities to fight hand-to-hand with the enemy.

b. Physical drill or exercises of some form should be scheduled at least six days a week during the entire training period. The exercises combined with hikes and field work will keep the men in good shape, and will improve their muscle tone and endurance. Some of the exercises are body-building, but since the program is designed for the average man, not every man will get the same benefit from them. However, all men will reach a fairly high common plane of strength and endurance.

c. It is essential that the men learn how to handle their bodies and learn good footwork, rolls and falls, as early as possible. As recruits, the men must accustom themselves to physical contact with the deck and with each other. This is usually accomplished by physical exercises and games where the men work against each other, and by elementary Judo and bayonet exercises.

d. A Combat Conditioning program should be progressive both in teaching and in practicing bayonet work, in disarming, and in Judo fundamentals and techniques. Only the most practicable and easily learned techniques should be

1

taught. The aggressive spirit must be inculcated from the beginning and developed throughout. At any stage of a Marine's training there are only a limited number of hours available for Combat Conditioning. However, if the fundamentals are taught first and the refinements later, and if both are practiced whenever possible, the limited time should not impair the opportunities of a combat conditioning program.

e. The Combat Conditioning program at Officer Candidates' School comprises eighteen hours of scheduled instruction, and three hours of physical drill, hikes, combat conditioning or work over the obstacle courses weekly during each of the twelve weeks of the course. We realize that the time allotted is not enough for us to teach you all the techniques that might well be taught or to allow you sufficient practice. Nor have we enough time devoted to combat conditioning to keep you in excellent physical condition at all times. We, of course, want to keep you in as good physical condition as possible while you are here, but our primary aim is to teach you combat conditioning and close combat techniques, and show you how you can teach others. All the essential techniques can be taught and absorbed in the time available here—a total of 54 hours.

f. Most of you Candidates have previously had about twenty hours of bayonet, Judo, and general physical training at recruit camp, and some of you have had more experience elsewhere. Actually the program used at OCS could be applied directly to new recruits if about two or three times as many hours were allotted for it. All extraneous or superfluous material has been excluded from the course. If recruits were to finish the expanded course, they would have acquired good physical condition, agility, and the aggressive spirit and would be able to use the bayonet effectively in combat. For recruit training purposes, of course, there would be no need for emphasis on training systems or methods of instruction.

(Notes for Instructors.)

3. **Program, Administration.**—The Combat Conditioning program in effect at the Officer Candidates' School is shown in outline on pages 4-12 as a suggested guide for similar programs. The instruction generally comes in the afternoon in two consecutive fifty-minute periods. The general plan of the course is explanation and demonstration by the officers and noncommissioned officers of the Combat Conditioning Section followed by practice under supervision of the officers and noncommissioned officer instructors of the company undergoing the instruction. The company instructors also conduct the competitive games and exercises and run their Candidates through the bayonet and obstacle course when scheduled. When a public address system is available it has been found expedient to give much of the bayonet instruction and drill

to the company as a unit. The company is placed in an extended formation and one instructor conducts the drill from the microphone while the other instructors circulate within their platoons, make any corrections necessary, and assist in any other ways possible. The uniform for all hands is dungarees.

4. **Equipment Used.**—a. The following equipment is used in the various phases of training:

(1) **Physical drill.**—Rifles, Pine Logs, twenty-five feet long and six inches to one foot in diameter. Abdominal Rise (situps) Rail—a wooden rail, padded with canvas, 100 feet long and 3½ feet high.

(2) **Judo and "deck" work.**—A sawdust pit approximately 80' by 100'.

(3) **Club.**—Wooden clubs two feet long and 1¼" in diameter.

(4) **Pistol.**—Dummy wooden pistols, same size as the Automatic Pistol, Caliber .45, M1911.

(5) **Knife.**—M1 Bayonets, with scabbards affixed.

(6) **Bayonet.**—Surveyed M1903 rifles, M1 bayonets, and surveyed wooden M1903 scabbards cut down to fit the M1 bayonets. (Surveyed rifles are used instead of M1 rifles since no protective front sight covers are available for the M1's and because the M1 bayonet scabbard splinters when used for bayonet practice. We have taken the long, surveyed M1903 wooden scabbards, cut them down, and taped them. Scabbards are fixed for all bayonet work except the running of the various obstacle and bayonet courses.)

(7) **Obstacle and bayonet courses.**—There are four courses, each different from the others. All except the first one of these are run with rifles and bayonets.

(8) **Obstacle course.**—The obstacle course for the individual man involves: weight lifting by rope and pulley; rope climbing; cargo net descent; stepping high and fast over criss-crossed logs; scaling a wall; traversing a horizontal rope hand over hand; stepping in and out of staggered boxes in rows while on the double; running across a straddle run (two 6' x 20' walls forming a "V" at the bottom and representing the deck of a heaving ship); running through vertical hatchways; hurdling two low and two high track hurdles; running across a long sand pit; and duck-waddling a certain distance. This course is run quite frequently by the Candidates. See Figure 20.

(9) **Bayonet course.**—The course is run on the double by individuals with rifle and bayonet. The details are shown on pages 289-295. This course is run a total of about six times by Candidates on three different days. See Figure 103.

3

(10) **Bayonet and assault course.**—Built entirely from natural materials. This course is also run on the double by individuals with rifle, bayonet, pack, and steel helmets. Its obstacles are similar to those shown in FM 23-25 (Bayonet). They include barbed wire fences and tunnels; log ramps and walls; standing, prone, and swinging brush dummies; foxholes and shell holes; and a water jump. This course is run three times.

(11) **Combat conditioning course.**—Also built from natural materials. Run on the double by four-man teams. Equipment is rifle, bayonet, belt, and steel helmet. Details are shown on pages 299-324. See Figures 104-118 inclusive. The course is run from two to a dozen times, as schedules permit.

b. Additional equipment consists of two mock-ups, each with four hatches, through which are passed two twenty-foot hand ropes and two twenty-foot, Navy, steel, chain-and-pipe ladders. Each mock-up is also provided with a 12", 20' x 20' landing net. Experience has shown that it is impossible for Marines to get too much practice climbing up and down landing nets. A guard rail around three sides of the platform is provided. No wooden or steel ladder is provided to the top, so that the men must climb a rope ladder or a cargo net in order to reach the top. A ladder could, however, be provided to expedite inspection of the knots and the platform. See Figure 119, page 325.

5. a. **Outline of Combat Conditioning Program (As a Guide for Instructors).**

All Instruction is in Field   Total Hours—Eighteen

Hour of Instr.	Scope	Type of Instruction	Equipment	Study Reference
1	MASS PHYSICAL DRILL. —Orientation, forming for and conduct of Physical Drill.	Brief lecture by a company instructor to his company.	None.	FM 21-20 Ch. 2, Sections I & V.
	Accelerated Calisthenics, Physical Drill under Arms, and slow and heavy exercises.	Two companies. Explanation and demonstration by Combat Conditioning Section. Execution by men in unison.	1 Portable Loudspeaker. 1 M1 Rifle per man.	LFM, 18-1, 18-2, 18-3, Combat Conditioning. Sections 1 & 2. LFM, Ch. 18, Section III.

4

Hour of Instr.	Scope	Type of Instruction	Equipment	Study Reference
2	OBSTACLE COURSE.— (25 min.) Layout, Required Actions, Conduct of Course (1st Phase)	Explanation and demonstration by Company Instructors. Practice by Candidates.	None.	Combat Conditioning, Section 2, par. 11.
	COMBAT CONDITIONING.—(25 min.) Introduction. Orientation. Rolls (front, back, & shoulder); falls (back and side); footwork. (2d Phase)	Explanation and demonstration by CC Section. Practice by the men in platoon sawdust pits.	1 Portable Loudspeaker.	Combat Conditioning, Section 3, par. 12.
3	WORKOUT.—Rolls and Falls as Warmup.	Practice by the men.	None.	All previous.
	JUDO.—Introduction to and brief history of Judo. Dirty fighting. Vital spots. How to disable and kill.	Brief lecture and demonstration by CC Section. Practice by the men and supervised by company officers and NCO's.	1 Portable Loudspeaker.	Combat Conditioning, Section 3, par. 13. FM 21-150, Sections I & II.
	TAKEDOWNS.—(1) Hip Throw, (2) Hip Throw Variation, (3) Rear Leg Trip.			
4	TAKEDOWNS.—The Hip Throw and Rear Leg Trip. (4) Front Leg Trip, (5) Drop Kick, (6) Belt Pull, (7) Body Pickup, (8) Alternative Body Pickup, and (9) Tackle.	Review by CC Section. Explanation and demonstration by CC Section. Practice by men in platoon areas.	1 Portable Loudspeaker.	All previous. Combat Conditioning, Section 3, par. 13 & 14.
	WORKOUT.—Circle Drill.	Explanation and demonstration by platoon instructors. Practice by platoons.	None.	Combat Conditioning, Section 5, par. 23.

Hour of Instr.	Scope	Type of Instruction	Equipment	Study Reference
5	WORKOUT.—(Three phases each of six minutes): (1) Abdominal Rises; (2) Rolls, falls, duck waddle and pushups; (3) obstacle course.	Conducted by platoons.	None.	All previous.
	JUDO. — Strangle and Breaks. General, Japanese Strangle. Escapes from Japanese Strangle: (1) Crotch Blow; (2) Trip; (3) Work on fingers.	Explanation and demonstration CC Section. Practice by company in platoon areas.	None.	Combat Conditioning, Section 3, par. 15.
6	JUDO.—Strangle Breaks, Breaks from forearm Strangle: (1) Crotch Blow, (2) Leg Trip, (3) Flying Mare, (4) Hammer Lock. From front Hand Strangle: (1) Crotch Blow, (2) Hand Wedge, Wrists Throws, (3) Left, (4) Right.	Explanation and demonstration by CC Section. Practice by company in platoon areas.	None.	Combat Conditioning, Section 3, par. 16. FM 21-150, Section V.
	Break from Bear Hug from Front: (1) Hit Vital Spots. From Rear, Arms free: (1) Flying Mare, (2) Switch. From Rear, Arms Trapped: (1) Crotch Blow and (2) Leg Trip.	Explanation and demonstration by CC Section. Practice by company in platoon areas.	None.	Combat Conditioning, Section 3, par. 16. FM 21-150, Section IV.
	MUSCLE STRUMMING.— Strumming chest, neck and back muscles.	Explanation and demonstration by CC Section. Practice by company in platoon areas.	None.	Combat Conditioning, Section 3, par. 16.

Hour of Instr.	Scope	Type of Instruction	Equipment	Study Reference
	COME - ALONGS.—(1) Thumb Catch Come-Along, (2) Handshake Come-Along, and (3) Hand Trick.	Explanation and demonstration by CC Section. Practice by company in platoon areas (if time permits.)	None.	Combat Conditioning, Section 3, par. 16. FM 21-150, Section IV.
7	PISTOL.—Use of the pistol; searching of prisoners; pistol disarming from the front: parry left or right, Hit Crotch (1,2) and Wrist Throw (3,4). From Rear: parry left or right, Hit Crotch (1,2) and Arm Lock (3,4) Disarming from the front: (1) Scissor Break and (2) Trigger Finger Break.	Explanation and demonstration by CC Section.	1 wooden dummy pistol per two men.	Combat Conditioning, Section 4, pars. 17, 18, 19, 20. FM 21-150, Section X.
	SILENT WEAPONS.—Garrote, Axe, Black-Jack, and Machete.	Explanation and demonstration by CC Section.	1 Garrote, 1 Axe, 1 Black-jack, 1 Machete 1 wooden club per two men	Combat Conditioning, Section 4, par. 21. Combat Conditioning, Section 4, par. 22. FM 21-150, Section IX.
	CLUB.—General; the long hold, the short hold; disarming with the club; club fighting; club come-alongs.	Explanation and demonstration by CC Section. Supervised practice by company in platoon areas.		

Hour of Instr.	Scope	Type of Instruction	Equipment	Study Reference
8	**WORKOUT.** — (Three phases each of ten minutes) (1) Abdominal rises; (2) obstacle course; (3) dives, rolls, and falls. Pushups and knee bends; rooster and horseback fights. Inter-platoon relay foot-race.	Practical work conducted by platoons, platoon instructors in charge.	None.	Combat Conditioning, Section 5, par. 23.
		Practical work conducted by company instructors.	None.	
9.	**KNIFE.**—Use of the knife; types of knives; grip and stance for knife fighting; where to strike; knife strokes; the thrust and the slash; knife attack. Taking down a sentry from behind.	Explanation and demonstration by CC Section. Supervised practice by company in platoon areas.	1 M1 Bayonet w/scabbard per man, 1 Portable loudspeaker, 1 Service Knife, 1 Stilletto, & 1 Machete for demonstration.	Combat Conditioning, Section 6, par. 25.
	KNIFE DEFENSE. — Defense against attack. Knife disarming. Defense against overhand stab w/cross Wrist Parry: (1) Grab Knife Wrist, Hit Crotch; (2) Grab with Right Hand-Wristlock; (3) Grab Wrist, Elbow Break, (4) Grab Wrist with Left Arm, Arm Lock. Forearm Parries: (1) Right Forearm, Wrist Lock; (2) Left Forearm, Wrist Lock.	Explanation and demonstration by CC Section. Supervised practice by company in platoon areas.	1 M1 Bayonet w/scabbard per two men.	Combat Conditioning, Section 6, par. 25. FM 23-25, Section IV, par. 16, 18. FM 21-150, Section VIII.
10	**WORKOUT.** — (Three phases each of six minutes): Abdominal rises; obstacle course; crab drill, pushups.	Practical work conducted by platoon.		

8

Hour of Instr.	Scope	Type of Instruction	Equipment	Study Reference
	KNIFE DISARMING.— Disarming for straight knife thrusts: (1) Step to Side, Elbow Break; (2) Step-to-Side, Hammer Lock. Disarming for a Side Thrust: (1) Parry out, Knee Crotch; Parry In— (2) Elbow Break or (3) Hammer Lock. Defense against an Underhand Stab: (1) Cross-Wrist Parry, Hammer Lock; (2) Double Hand Catch, Arm Drag, Knee Crotch.	Explanation and demonstration by CC Section. Supervised practice by company in platoon areas.	1 M1 Bayonet w/scabbard per two men.	Combat Conditioning, Section 6, par. 26.
11	BAYONET. — Introduction to course of bayonet. Theory of the bayonet. Bayonet technique; grip, stance, footwork, whirls, thrusts, buttstrokes, and straight parries.	Explanation and demonstration by CC Section. Controlled practice by platoons.	1 M1 Rifle, 1 M1 bayonet per man. 1 Portable Loudspeaker.	Combat Conditioning, Section 7, par. 27. FM 23-25, Section I & II, Section V (20a,b).
12	BAYONET.—Rolling with rifle and bayonet. Footdrill. Continue thrust and buttstroke sequences and foot-drill.	Explanation and demonstration by CC Section. Practice by company in sawdust pit. Controlled practice by platoons.	1 M1 Rifle and 1 M1 Bayonet per man.	Combat Conditioning, Section 7, par. 28.
13	WORKOUT WITH RIFLES.—(Three phases each of five minutes): Vaulting rail; hurdling ditch; and rolling. Review work of 12th hour. Thrust and buttstroke sequences worked in with foot-drill.	Controlled practical work by platoons. Explanation and demonstration by CC Section. Controlled practice by platoons.	1 M1 Rifle and 1 M1 bayonet per man. 1 Portable Loudspeaker.	All previous. Combat Conditioning, Section 7, par. 29.

Hour of Instr.	Scope	Type of Instruction	Equipment	Study Reference
	Hand Signals.	Supervised practice by pairs in platoon areas.	1 M1 Rifle and 1 M1 Bayonet w/scabbard per two men.	
14	WORKOUT.—Wheelbarrow Race, inter-platoon.	Practical work conducted by company instructors.	1 Portable Loudspeaker.	
	BAYONET.—The shift parry, right and left, used both offensively and defensively. Bayonet Course.	Explanation and demonstration by CC Section. Controlled practice by platoons. Explanation and demonstration by CC Section. Supervised practical work, (run through by each individual).	1 M1 Rifle and 1 M1 Bayonet w/scabbard.	Combat Conditioning, Section 7, par. 30. Combat Conditioning, Section 7, par. 30.
15	BAYONET.—Review Shift Parry, right and left. The variations to the shift parry: Deck Parry, Double Parry; Miss; and Disengage.	Explanation and demonstration by CC Section. Controlled practice by half of company in bayonet formation (4 ranks); supervised practice in pairs.	1 surveyed 1903 Rifle, M1 Bayonet and surveyed M1903 scabbard per man.	Combat Conditioning, Section 7, par. 31.

Hour of Instr.	Scope	Type of Instruction	Equipment	Study Reference
16	BAYONET.—Manipulation moves: Reverse; Change over; Square Guard, Squat Guard, and respective parries. The feints: Front-Pass - and Throw; Gain-Point - High - Slash - Low; Gain - Point - Low - Slash-High.	Explanation and demonstration by CC Section. Controlled practice by half of company in pairs and then supervised practice in pairs.	1 surveyed 1903 Rifle, M1 Bayonet, and surveyed M1903 scabbard per man.	Combat Conditioning, Section 7, par. 32.
	Bayonet Course.	Supervised practical work. (Run through by all individuals).		
17	BAYONET. — Review of previous work; (two phases, each of 15 minutes): Judo; Bayonet.	Explanation and demonstration by CC Section. Supervised practical work by half of company on each phase.	1 surveyed 1903 Rifle, M1 Bayonet, and surveyed M1903 scabbard per man. 1 portable loudspeaker.	All previous.
	Group Assault Tactics: theory; two vs. one; one vs. two; three vs. two; and two vs. three.	Explanation by CC Section. Demonstration by company instructors. Practice by company in platoon areas, closely supervised.		Combat Conditioning, Section 7, par. 33. FM 23-25, Section III.

Hour of Instr.	Scope	Type of Instruction	Equipment	Study Reference
18	BAYONET.—Team tactics fighting.	Selected candidates demonstration, interplatoon competition. One man, 1st platoon vs. two men, 2d platoon; three men, 3d platoon vs. two men, 1st platoon.	1 surveyed M1903 Rifle, 1 M1 Bayonet and 1 M1903 scabbard per man. 1 Portable Loudspeaker.	All previous. Combat Conditioning, Section 7, par. 34.
	BAYONET DISARMING.—Orientation, disarming technique from the front; (1) Parry left, over the shoulder; (2) Parry down, twist-away, From the rear —Parry left; over the shoulder.	Explanation and demonstration by CC Section.	1 surveyed M1903 Rifle, M1 Bayonet, and surveyed M1903 scabbard per two men.	All previous.
	JAPANESE BAYONET TECHNIQUE: Basic thrusts, slashes, butt strokes, parries, feints and tactics.	Demonstration by CC Section.	1 Japanese uniform, 1 Japanese helmet, 1 Japanese rifle, 1 Japanese bayonet, 1 M1 Rifle, 1 M1 Bayonet.	

b.   The schedule is flexible and depends upon how much previous instruction the Candidates have had, and how quickly the instruction is absorbed.

c.   The most essential moves and techniques are always taught first, then, if there is more time available, less essential techniques are taught. The scheduled workouts and competitive games are flexible and can be expanded or cut down on, as the occasion demands.

SECTION 2

MASS PHYSICAL DRILL

6. General.—a. Mass physical drill is a tried-and-true method of giving a relatively large number of men physical exercise with minimum confusion, in a minimum of time, and with minimum space and equipment requirements. Mass physical drills have certain definite advantages and disadvantages for conditioning purposes.

b. The chief advantages are:

(1) Large numbers of men can obtain a good physical workout at the same time.

(2) The time required is relatively short.

(3) The space required is relatively small.

(4) No equipment is required (other than organic weapons and equipment which will be used occasionally to supplement and improve some of the exercises).

(5) The drill may be given from close order formations and can be administered by a relatively small number of instructors with minimum confusion.

c. The chief disadvantages are:

(1) Due to restricted lateral space men cannot gain the agility and endurance for running that they will need.

(2) The exercises are not inherently interesting.

(3) Unlimited all around physical development is impossible.

(4) Although certain physical drill exercises can condition the men to bodily contact, they neither create nor promote an aggressive spirit within the individual.

d. The exercises consist mainly of bending the body in various ways, moving the limbs and body in rhythm, and stretching and exerting the muscles. The individual muscle stretching and exertion is increased when certain of the exercises are done with arms or organic equipment such as rifles, machine guns, mortars, gun mounts, or loaded ammunition boxes. When the drill is conducted progressively by an instructor who can arouse enthusiasm among the men and lead them through the exercises in a vigorous manner, the men will be benefited appreciably by attaining a fairly good "wind" and good muscular tone and strength. It is essential that the men must want to do the exercises and have the spirit and energy to carry them out with a zest. Upon this point the success of any mass physical drill program hinges, and it is here that good leadership is at a premium. Once having aroused the interest of the men, the instructor can increase the speed of the exercises or the number of counts or both. In this way the men can increase their strength and endurance and will exercise on their "second wind." When possible every unit undergoing training should have progressive mass physical training.

e. Mass physical drill is an important part of the combat conditioning program for troops at every stage of training and should be used to the fullest whenever time and other conditions permit. The drill will be supplemented by bayonet work, by field work, and by running bayonet, assault, and obstacle courses. No one of these can do the job of physical conditioning alone. They are supplementary and are all essential. However, mass physical drill comes the closest to doing the whole job. The disadvantage that there can be no running is overcome to quite an extent by knee bends and stationary double time exercises. However, there is no real substitute for actual running in the field as far as combat conditioning goes. Aboard ship mass physical drill is often the only form of exercise available and, therefore, becomes doubly important. The best time to give the drill is in the afternoon or in the morning at least two hours after meals. It can be given in the early morning before breakfast, but the chances are that not much good will be derived from it at that time, as the men are inclined to be sleepy, hungry, and apathetic.

7. **Forming for Physical Drill.**—a. Forming for mass physical drill can be done in any way the company officers or noncommissioned officers desire. An easy way to form a company in a simple compact formation, from a column of platoons at close interval is to execute either "Company Mass Ten Paces Left (or Right)" or "Platoons Column Left (or Right)". From this formation the company executes:

(1) 1. Extend to the Left (or Right), 2. MARCH. The right squad (file) stands fast with arms extended sideward. The second and third squads from the right, turn to the left and taking up the double time, run forward to the original left, the second squad taking two paces interval and the third taking four paces. After taking the required distance, all face to the front, with arms extended sideward, the distance between the fingertips being about 12 inches.

(2) 1. Arms, 2. DOWN—The arms are lowered smartly to the sides. The men in each file are now covering in column at 40 inches distance and are too close to carry out the exercise.

(3) 1. Even Numbers to the Right (Left), 2. MOVE—Each even-numbered man stride-jumps to the right, squarely to the middle of the interval. In doing this he swings his right leg sideward, jumps from his left foot and lights on his right foot, bringing the left smartly into position against the right.

(4) To assemble, the instructor commands: 1. Assemble, 2. MARCH. At the command "MARCH" all return to their original position in column on the double.

14

b. Forming the company in the above manner will put the men in a formation that is roughly square. Where lateral space is limited as on shipboard the company can be formed directly for physical drill from a column of threes, or, if necessary, from a column of twos.

8. **Conducting Mass Physical Drill.**—a. Physical Drill is conducted by an instructor of good voice and physique who can execute and conduct all exercises correctly and vigorously. He leads the drill from a raised platform or other position where he can see the entire company and where all the men can see him. His personality should convey enthusiasm and force to the men. He designates the exercise, demonstrates it if necessary, and then leads the men through it, performing the exercise with them or interrupting his own exercising, as necessary, to observe the men or to make corrections. As soon as the men have learned the names of and manner of execution of the exercises, the instructor eliminates the demonstration. He will allow less and less resting time between exercises as the men's "wind" improves. He may have an assistant or one of the men execute the exercises up on the platform while he circulates around observing the men at work, but he will still control the drill by his commands.

b. **Commands.**—(1) His commands are simple. He designates the exercise, initiates it by a command of execution, regulates it by counting, and halts it by another command. With some exercises the company counts out loud in unison as the exercise is executed.

(2) **For Physical Drill Under Arms.**—(An exercise still universal in the Marine Corps) the instructor calls the men to the "Ready" position (left foot moved 18 inches to the left, rifle held across the chest with the right hand at the small of the stock, left hand at the upper hand guard, palms to the front and rifle sling up).

(3) His commands are: 1. Come to the Ready, 2. ONE, 3. TWO, 4. THREE.

(4) His commands are for the first exercise: 1. Down and Forward, 2. ONE, TWO, THREE, FOUR, ONE, etc. He repeats the count four times and on the last set of four counts substitutes 1. Company (Battalion), 2. HALT for "ONE, TWO." The men halt the exercise in two counts just as they halt in two counts from the march. As an alternative the physical drill conductor can give, 1. Battalion, 2. HALT instead of "THREE, FOUR." This is recommended when the exercise is a relatively slow one. Whichever method the instructor uses to halt an exercise, he should employ that method exclusively for all exercises.

(5) For **Accelerated Calisthenics** the commands are: "The First (Next) Exercise is the Side-Straddle Hop executed in four counts as follows:" (Demonstrate a few times). "Sixteen Counts, Slow; Sixteen Counts, Fast. All Hands

15

Count. 1. Ready, 2. BEGIN. ONE, TWO, THREE, Etc."
The men will then execute the Side Straddle Hop sixteen times
in unison and then sixteen times as fast as they can. The
rhythm for drill in unison is approximately 140 counts per
minute.

(6) For **Slow and Heavy Exercises** the starting
commands are similar to those used for accelerated calisthenics.
The instructor will lead the men through the exercise by
counting as long as he thinks it desirable. He halts them as he
did in the Physical Drill under Arms.

(7) There is a simple variation of the manner of
counting which can be used to stimulate men to further effort
in physical drill. Instead of counting, "ONE, TWO, THREE,
FOUR, etc.", the instructor counts, "ONE, TWO, THREE,
FOUR; ONE, TWO, THREE, **TWO**; ONE, TWO, THREE,
THREE, Etc.," thus announcing as the last count the total
number of times the movement has been done. This gives the
men an idea how many times they have done the particular
exercise. The instructor should remind the men how many
times they did the exercise the day before and encourage them
to increase the total number of times executed from day to
day. Having the men count as they execute an exercise will
often increase their interest in the work.

9. **Mass Physical Drill Programs.**—1st Hour of Officer Candidates' School Combat Conditioning Program; Introduction to
Physical Drill.

a. The company is assembled on the pavement in the
vicinity of the barracks and formed for physical drill by company instructors, companies abreast and centered in front of
platform.

b. An instructor of the Combat Conditioning Section
gives the men an introduction as follows: You are now in
the formation for physical drill which you will use out here
during most of the early morning periods in Officer Candidates'
School. As part of your schedules here, there is a twenty
minute workout period before breakfast each day of the week.
The exercises include light "loosening-up" exercises, "heavy"
exercises, accelerated exercises, and drill under arms. Some of
you are familiar with many of these exercises already.

c. Fifteen minutes every morning is too short a time to
get much out of these drills physically unless you carry out
the exercises with a lot of pep. We start work out here at
0540 and knock off at 0600, which gives you time to get ready
for chow. If you put everything you have into the exercises,
you will stay in pretty good shape throughout the course, and
if you keep your eyes and ears open, you will know how to give
physical drill to your own men at some future date. We expect
every man to take this work seriously. We want every man to
know how to form a company for physical drill and how to lead
it in physical drill.

d. **The schedule calls for:**

Monday: Accelerated Calisthenics.

Tuesday: Slow and Heavy Exercises Without Arms.

Wednesday: Physical Drill Under Arms and Without Arms.

Thursday: Air Bedding and Double Time.

Friday: Slow and Heavy Exercises Without Arms.

Saturday: Combination of Accelerated and Slow Exercises.

e. We will run through the exercises now and let you see how they are done.

At this point the Officer in Charge leads the battalion through all exercises used, one by one, demonstrating each one before the companies perform it. The Candidates will do the exercises in half the prescribed number of counts. Heavy and light exercises will be well mixed so that the men will not strain themselves or get too tired.

f. Company instructors will check on the men to see that they perform exercises correctly. The method prescribed for forming for physical drill and the manner of conducting and performing physical drill and drill with and without arms will be made known to the Candidates by their company officers prior to the first assembly for such drills.

g. **Exercises should be given in order indicated:** (Refer to Par. 10a, **Physical Drill Definitions**, Section 2, page 20.)

Accelerated Calisthenics:	Instructor Emphasizes
1. Stationary Double Time	Knees raised at least as high as hips.
2. Side Straddle Hop	
3. Breathing Exercise	(1) Stretch fingers and arms upward to the utmost, inhaling deeply, way off toes. (2) drop down on heels—hold breath while pounding chest or stomach.
4. Side Straddle Bend	(1) Keep knees straight, bend from waist, touch fingers to deck; (2) Stand straight up again.
5. Stomach and Leg	Keep heels off the deck when on back. Contract stomach muscles.
6. Grasp wrist under knee	Bend down and forward, rear leg well extended; **grasp** wrist each time.
7. Pushups (B)	

8.	Windmill	Keep arms stretched straight out at all times; turn only from the waist and hip; keep feet flat on the deck. For slow counts execute exercise in (4) counts, straightening up after each bend. For fast counts execute in (2) counts staying bent over.
9.	Backward Kick	Stretch leg to rear as far as possible.
10.	Breathing Exercise	Good as a "break" from the heavier exercises.
11.	Spread Eagle	Keep heels off the deck, arms and legs straight.
12.	Pairs:	
	(a) Fireman's Carry, Deep Knee Bend	Go "all the way down."
	(b) Hands Locked	
	(c) Back-to-back	
	(d) Bulling	Stay low and push hard—force your partner to the deck.
	(e) Rowing	Both men must have feet well drawn up when in position. Pull way back.

h. Slow and Heavy:

1.	Front Lean	
2.	Deep Knee Bend	(1) Feet flat—go way down; (2) keep knees straight, bend down from waist, touch deck.
3.	Stomach, Legs Circling	Keep legs straight.
4.	Pushups (A)	Keep back straight.

i. Under Arms:		(Caution men to stay with the count, make movements snappy, stretch muscles).
Come to the Ready		(Preparatory Command); "ONE." (Command of Execution), "TWO," etc.
1.	Down and Forward	Touch rifle to the deck when "Down."
2.	Forward and Up	
3.	Up and On Shoulders	Keep head high and erect, stretch shoulders.
4.	Side Pushes	
5.	Forward Lunge	Arms straight, way over head.

6.	Deep Breathing	Let air out slowly 3 times; rapidly with yell (2) times.
7.	Diagonal Lunges	
8.	Front Sweeps Slow	Keep arms and legs straight at all times. Touch deck when "down," stretch arm, back, and leg muscles.
9.	Overhead, B u t t s and Muzzles, Alternate	
10.	Side Twists	Keep body straight, but stretch arm, back, and shoulder muscles.

ORDER ARMS—GROUND ARMS

j. Slow and Heavy Exercises:

1.	Bicycle	Stay well up on shoulder blades.
2.	Stomach from Sitting Position	Don't combine any of the (4) separate movements with each other. Do them precisely or no good is obtained from the exercise.
3.	Arm Straddle	Actually straddle the arm.
4.	Body Twist	Keep feet in place on deck.
5.	Stomach Twist	Touch feet to deck. Keep arms outspread and shoulders on the deck.

k. **Program Arrangement.**—In any physical drill program there should be a variety of exercises to tone and develop all the major muscles of the body—i.e., the muscles of the arms, legs, chest, back, sides, abdomen, shoulders, and neck. Many exercises will contract and release several different sets of muscles. If possible the workout each day should exercise all or most of the muscles, especially the ones that are needed most by the individual Marine in field work. Some exercises, the slow and heavy ones in particular, involve a good deal of positive muscular work. Others such as the accelerated calisthenics and physical drill under arms involve less positive muscular work and are more suitable for all easy limbering and stretching of the muscles. The latter exercises are used in conjunction with slow and heavy exercises both for the sake of variety and to avoid muscular overtone or fatigue. The daily exercise schedule is arranged with this in mind. For each day the exercises should always be arranged so that the light ones come first, giving the men a chance to "warm up" before the heavier ones. When heavy exercises are involved, it is generally best to have the extremity (arm and leg) work precede the body (trunk) work. One day "off" per week is recommended both to prevent staleness and to allow the body to rest and repair itself, especially when the physical work has been strenuous and extensive.

10. Physical Drill Definitions.—a. Stationary Double Time. —See Figure 1.

Start out slowly, feet raised well off the deck, with plenty of swinging of the arms or clapping the hands. After a half minute, speed up as fast as possible for half a minute. Very good to start the routine, as it gets all hands loosened up and breathing well.

R.D. 4443

Figure 1.—Stationary Double Time.

R.D. 4443

Figure 2.—Side Straddle Hop.

b.   **Side Straddle Hop.**—(See Figure 2).

Start from position of standing with feet together and arms at side.

1.   On the count of "one" spread feet wide apart and bring arms together overhead.

2.   On the count of "two," arms down and feet together.

With the Side Straddle Hop, as with all accelerated calisthenics, all hands count out loud and consecutively, one count for each movement. Sixteen counts slow and sixteen counts fast.

21

c. **Breathing Exercise.**—(See Figures 3a, b, c).
Three counts—executed six times.

1. Up on toes, arms raised overhead, inhale.
2. Arms down, pound on chest with closed fists while holding breath.
3. Exhale with loud yell.

Executed three times pounding on chest and three times pounding on stomach.

R.D. 4443

Figure 3(a).—Deep Breathing—Part 1.

R.D. 4443

Figure 3(b).—Deep Breathing—Part 2.

R.D. 4443

Figure 3(c).—Deep Breathing—Part 3.

Figure 4.—Side Straddle Bend.

d. **Side Straddle Bend.**—(Figure 4).

Same as Side Straddle Hop except that instead of raising arms overhead, bend down and touch the deck. All hands count out loud, sixteen counts slow and sixteen counts fast.

e. **Stomach and Leg Exercises.**—(Figures 5a, b).

Two counts—executed ten times. The starting position is on the back, heels raised six inches off deck.

1. Draw in legs and raise body bringing knees and chest together, clasp arms around knees, and pull tight.

2. Straighten out body, but do not touch heels to deck.

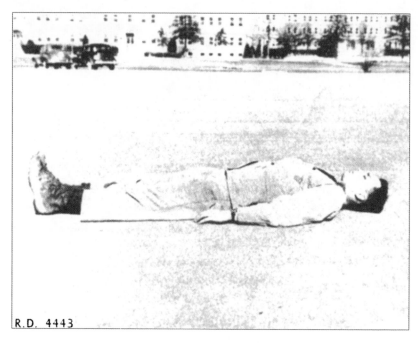

Figure 5(a).—Stomach and Leg—Part 1.

R.D. 4443

Figure 5(b).—Stomach and Leg—Part 2.

f. **Grasping Wrist Under Knee.**—(Figure 6).
Starting position, standing.

      1. Left foot well forward, right foot back; bend way down, arms around left knee grasping left wrist with right hand.

      2. Right foot forward, left foot back and grasp right wrist under right knee.

Two counts—sixteen slow and sixteen rapidly with all hands counting.

Figure 6.—Grasp Wrists Under Knees.

g. **Push Ups.**—(Figure 7).

Six counts, executed ten times, slow count.

    1.   Hands on deck in front of feet and about two feet apart.

    2.   Feet to the rear so that body rests on hands and toes, back straight.

    3.   Body lowered so chest only touches deck, keep back straight.

    4.   Push up to full extent of arms.

    5.   Feet under body.

    6.   Stand up.

This exercise may be executed in one count. The starting position is prone with hands flat on deck alongside of shoulders. At (1) push up vigorously so that entire body, including feet, is off deck.

Clap hands together and settle back to starting position. Repeat ten times.

Figure 7.—Pushups Type "B".

h. **Windmill Exercise.**—(Figures 8a, b).

Position: Standing, feet spread, arms out to sides.

Four counts, all hands count, sixteen slow and sixteen fast.

1. Bend and touch right foot with left hand.
2. Straighten up to starting position.
3. Touch left foot with right hand.
4. Back to starting position.

R.D. 4443

Figure 8(a).—Windmill—Part 1.

R.D. 4443

Figure 8(b).—Windmill—Part 2.

i.   **Backward Kicking.**—(Figure 9).

Position: Stooped, with hands on deck in front of feet.

   1.   Kick left leg to the rear.

   2.   Left leg drawn in under body. Repeat for eight counts 1-2, 3-4, 5-6, 7-8. Then eight counts right leg. Then sixteen alternating left and right legs at each count. All hands count.

j.   **Spread Eagle.**—(Figure 10).

Position on back, legs together, arms at sides. Heels off deck. Two counts, twenty slow, all hands count.

   1.   Spread out arms and legs.

   2.   Arms alongside body, legs together.

R.D. 4443

Figure 9.—Backward Kick.

R.D. 4443

Figure 10.—Spread Eagle.

k. **Front Lean Exercise.**—(Figures 11a, b).
Start from standing. Four counts—repeat ten times.
    1.   Hands on deck just in front of feet.
    2.   Feet to rear so body rests on hands and toes, back straight.
    3.   Feet drawn in under body.
    4.   Stand up.

R.D. 4443

Figure 11(a).—Front Lean—Part 1.

Figure 11(b).—Front Lean—Part 2.

l. **Deep Knee Bend.**—(Figures 12a, b).
Start from standing, feet apart and flat, hands on hips.
Four counts. Repeat ten times.

1. Squat, full knee bend, feet flat, arms raised horizontally to front.

2. Arms down, stand up.

3. Bend forward from waist, touch deck, knees straight.

4. Starting position.

Figure 12(a).—Deep Knee Bend—Part 1.

R.D. 4443

Figure 12(b).—Deep Knee Bend—Part 2.

m. **Stomach Exercise From Sitting.**—(Figures 13a, b, c).

Starting position—sitting.
Four counts—repeat ten times.

  1. Lower back to deck. (Do not raise legs).
  2. Raise legs to vertical position.
  3. Legs down to deck.
  4. Raise body to sitting position.

n. **Stomach Twist.**—(Figure 14).

Starting position on back with legs raised to vertical position, and arms straight out from shoulders and flat on deck.

Four counts—repeat ten times.

    1.   Twist lower body to left so legs touch deck, legs stiff and together.

    2.   Raise legs to vertical position.

    3.   Twist to right. Feet and legs touch deck.

    4.   Return to starting position.

R.D. 4443

Figure 13(a).—Stomach-Sitting—Part 1.

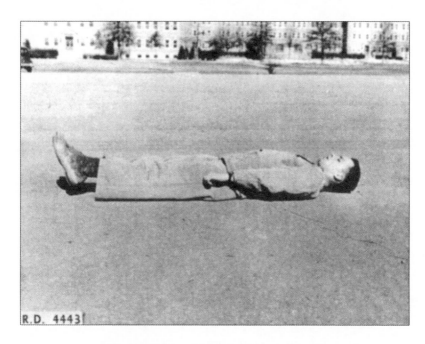

Figure 13(b).—Stomach-Sitting—Part 2.

Figure 13(c).—Stomach-Sitting—Part 3.

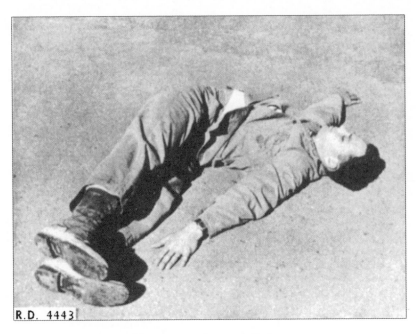

Figure 14.—Stomach Twist.

o. **Stomach Exercise—Legs Circling.**—(Figure 15).

Starting from position on back, feet together and raised six inches.

Two counts. Repeat ten times.

    1.   Spread legs wide apart and raise upward coming together in vertical position.

    2.   Lower legs keeping feet together.

This movement to be executed five times. Next five times start with legs up, feet together, and spread legs wide coming down.

p. **Arm Straddle.**—(Figure 16).

Excellent for working all muscles of the body. Eight counts—repeat ten times.

    1.   Hands on deck just in front of feet.

    2.   Legs and feet pushed to rear so body rests on hands and toes.

    3.   Legs drawn up under body so that left arm is straddled.

    4.   Feet pushed to rear.

    5.   Legs drawn up to straddle right arm.

    6.   Feet pushed to rear.

    7.   Legs drawn up under body.

    8.   Stand up.

Figure 15.—Stomach—Legs Circling.

Figure 16.—Arm Straddle.

41

q. **Body Twist.**—(Figure 17).

Starting position—standing. Eight counts—repeat ten times. Slow count first few times.

1. Hands on deck just in front of feet.

2. Feet pushed to rear and well apart. Back straight.

3. Twist body to right bringing left hand over to touch deck on right side.

4. Back to #2 position.

5. Twist body to left bringing right hand over to touch deck on left side.

6. Back to #2 position.

7. Feet under body.

8. Stand up·

While twisting body, keep feet apart and on deck.

r. **Bicycle Exercise.**—(Figure 18).

Position: Body nearly vertical, supported on shoulders, back of neck and upper arms. Feet in air, hands supporting buttocks.

Exercise: "Pedal" vigorously with the feet in circles in a motion similar to riding a bicycle.

R.D. 4443

Figure 17.—Body Twist.

R.D. 4443

Figure 18.—Bicycle.

s. **Working in Pairs.—**

1. **Fireman's Carry—Deep Knee Bend** (Figure 19a).

Position: One man carrying the other with Fireman's Carry in standing position.

Exercise: Do five full deep knee bends and then change over for five more. This exercise can be executed with or without control by the Physical Drill Conductor.

2. **Hand Wrestling** (Figure 19b).

Position: Men opposite each other in crouched position, hands clenched, palm to palm.

Exercise: Then men try to wrestle each other off balance and to the deck using their hands only. This exercise is executed uncontrolled.

3. **Back-to-Back-Arms Locked** (Figure 19c).

Position: Men back to back with arms locked.

Exercise: First one man bends over, riding the other man up onto his back, and shakes him two or three times. Then the second man bends over and shakes the first man vigorously. Executed uncontrolled.

4. **Bulling Exercises** (Figure 19d).

Position: Men facing each other, just off the knees in a crawling position; one hand on the deck, the other arm around the other man's neck in a headlock.

Exercise: Bull your opponent around using your headlock on him, and try to force him over or onto the deck. Executed uncontrolled.

5. **Rowing Exercise** (Figure 19e).

Position: Men seated on the deck, facing each other with feet against opposite man's feet, finger interlocked, and arms out-stretched.

Exercise: One man pulls the other man towards him leaning way back as he does. The man being pulled resists strongly with his back and stomach. Then the second man pulls the first one towards him in like manner and the men alternate five or six times. Execute uncontrolled.

Figure 19(a).—Pairs, Fireman's Carry—Deep Knee Bend.

Figure 19(b).—Pairs, Hand Wrestling.

46

R.D. 4443

Figure 19(c).—Pairs, Back to Back, Arms Locked.

Figure 19(d).—Pairs, Bulling.

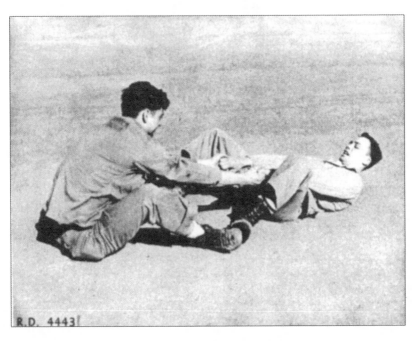

Figure 19(e).—Pairs, Rowing.

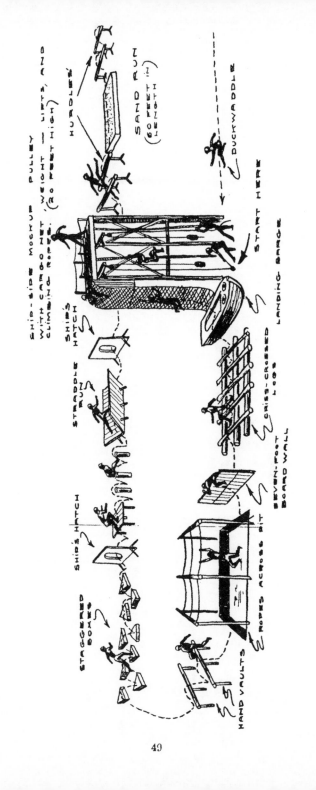

SHIP-SIDE MOCKUP PULLEY WITH CARGO NET, WEIGHT LIFTS, AND CLIMBING ROPES. (20 FEET HIGH)

HURDLES'

SAND RUN (60 FEET LENGTH)

DUCKWADDLE

START HERE

LANDING BARGE

SHIPS HATCH

STRADDLE RUN

CRISS-CROSSED LOGS

SEVEN-FOOT BOARD WALL

SHIPS HATCH

STAGGERED BOXES

ROPES ACROSS PIT

HAND VAULTS

49

OBSTACLE COURSE (Refer to Figure 20.)

11. Obstacle Course.—(Half hour obstacle course, half hour Combat Conditioning.)

a. The company will be lined up in a column of fours facing the obstacle course. A company instructor explains how to run through the obstacle course (while another instructor demonstrates): When you run this course you will normally run through it on the double, but today we'll take it easy to learn the methods correctly. You will move off from the column of fours one rank at a time, half going to the right side of the structure and half to the left. You will first pull one weight to the top and then switch over and pull up the other one. Be careful you don't hit someone on the head with the weights when you let them down. Then go inside the framework and climb one rope all the way to the top using your hands only. We want you to touch the top. You can use your legs if you can't make it with hands alone.

b. Next climb up the ladder, go across the platform and over the side, left leg over first. Come down the cargo net hand over hand with your feet away from the bulkhead and out of the net. You land in a landing barge. We want you to vault out of that barge without touching your feet to the rail at all. Then double time across the log obstacles putting your feet on the deck and **not** stepping on the logs. Without stopping, scale the wall by any means you can.

c. Then go the entire distance of the overhead ropes hand-over-hand and vault over the two rails; then turn right and come through the back leg of the course by running through the staggered rows of boxes, stepping into each one; jumping through the ship's hatch; jumping on and off of the bench; leap-frogging the poles; running the straddle run; jumping through the second ship's hatch; running the low and high hurdles and the sand run; and finishing off by duck-waddling 50-75 yards back to the starting point. After you have run this course once or twice you will see how you have to use every muscle in your body at some time or other. Since most men's shoulders and arms are weak in relation to their backs and legs, we give a heavy emphasis to arm and shoulder development at the very start of the course when the men are fresh. This of course is brought out in rope-climbing, weight pulling, cargo net descent, and hand-over-hand traversing of the horizontal rope. Then just when the men are getting pretty tired comes a lot of running to help develop endurance. The ship's hatches and the straddle run which represents a ship's heaving deck, are to help your balance and agility and at the same time possibly to acquaint you with a couple of conditions you may meet aboard ship some day. The sand run, you will agree, will exercise muscles in your feet and legs that you scarcely knew you had. Actually these are some of the muscles you need most in hill-and-dale climbing and in moving over swampy, sandy or 'loose' terrain.

d. The company instructors will then run the company through the course once (or twice if time permits). An instructor should be stationed at each obstacle to see that the Candidates go through it correctly. If there is a short period of time left, it will add interest to run the three platoons in competition in scaling the wall.

The total time for the company on the obstacle course should be about 25 minutes. After one company has run the course, companies change over.

JUDO

12. Introduction to Combat Conditioning Program, Second Hour.—The company will be assembled in a large circle in the sawdust square. Company instructors will be standing by and will observe the candidates when they practice a movement. They will be ready to assist the candidates, to instruct them, and to make corrections when necessary.

a. **Orientation.**—(1) The Company Combat Conditioning instructor will take charge of the assembled company and orient them: This is your first hour in physical training here in Officer Candidates School. You have eighteen hours scheduled. This includes eight hours of Judo and Disarming with rifle, pistol, or knife, and eight hours on work with the bayonet. The work we give you with Judo includes footwork, vital parts of the body, use of the fists, hands and feet in fighting, takedowns, breaks, and other movements of unarmed combat. We also teach you how to disarm an attacker armed with a rifle, pistol, or knife. In bayonet work you will learn footwork, thrusts, jabs, slashes, parries, and buttstrokes. We'll teach you a system of bayonet fighting which incorporates the best features of several well-known styles of bayonet fighting.

(2) The work is spread out very thinly over the entire course. It won't give you much time to master the techniques we will teach. You may forget them from one session to the next. For this reason you must give this work all the attention and applied energy that you've got; and you must ask questions about any of these movements you don't follow. A booklet will be issued to each man. This booklet contains all the material on the entire course. We want you to refer to them and to Physical Training and Bayonet Field Manuals. We want you to practice this stuff on your own time when you get a chance—in the squadroom, out here after hours, or whenever there is an opportunity. There is a reason why you should learn these techniques. Marines are traditionally tough fighting men. The Marine Corps emphasizes judo, disarming, and bayonet in all combat training. This training is good to harden men physically and to give them a lot of confidence in their abilities to close with the enemy—and from time to time it has come into practical use in combat. Where the Marines are fighting today combat has often ended up at very close range. There has been some hand-to-hand fighting. We fight the enemy first at long range with naval guns, planes, artillery, mortars, and machine guns but eventually we have to finish him with cold steel at close range. The thing is this—you're going to have to be ready to teach this stuff to your own troops some day and the more you work with this type of fighting the more confidence you will have in it and in yourself. You'll get out of it just as much as you

put into it. Let's stay awake and on the ball and really turn to. We'll have a little competition from time to time—tug o' war, relays and the like—so it won't be all work and no play.

That's enough for the introduction. Now today for a little basic work we are going to give you some footwork and also teach you how to fall and roll. First of all the roll.

b. **Rolls.**—We will demonstrate now how to roll. This is good for hardening men up—also it is a practical way to avoid the embarrassing consequences that might follow if you tripped and fell when you were running towards the enemy, for by using this roll you not only don't hurt yourself but immediately regain your feet and balance even if you're carrying a rifle.

Demonstration of the forward roll, slow.

(1)   **Front Roll.**—See Figures 20a, 20b, 20c.

Notice how he puts his hands on the deck, fingers pointing outboard to help break the fall, and that he lets his arms bend at the elbows. Now he lets his weight go well forward and ducks his head, kicking up his heels. He tucks his feet in, his body curled up like a ball. He lands on his back between his shoulder blades and rolls right over, his momentum carrying him back on to his feet.. His right foot should be tucked in more than his left so that when he lands on his feet, he'll be in a boxer's stance and ready to go.

Demonstrate several times, faster.

R.D. 4443

Figure 20(a).—Front Roll—Part 1.

54

Figure 20(b).—Front Roll—Part 2.

Figure 20(c).—Front Roll—Part 3.

55

(2) **Side Roll.**—That was the forward roll. Now some people find it easier to roll on their side with the so-called "side roll" or "shoulder roll". The hand or forearm breaks the fall the same way as before but the head is ducked to one side and down and the shoulder is dropped. You land on your shoulder blade and back and roll over on them as before, landing on your feet.

Demonstrate several times, faster.

(3) **Backward Roll.**—See Figures 21a, 21b, 21c.

A Marine must also know how to roll backwards in case he trips while moving backwards. The back roll is practically the reverse of the front roll but there are a few essential differences. When the person feels himself falling to the rear or if the roll is a practice one, he should squat down by bending his knees and at the same time helping to break his fall by placing his hands on the deck. He tucks his chin onto his chest and his feet leave the deck. His body again is curved back and also on his arms and elbows. He rolls over in one continuous motion onto the back of his neck and by helping with his hands lands on his feet in a crouched position. It is possible by rolling quite fast and pushing vigorously with the hands to land on one's feet in a standing position.

Demonstrate several times faster.

R.D. 4443

Figure 21(a).—Back Roll—Part 1.

56

Figure 21(b).—Back Roll—Part 2.

Figure 21(c).—Back Roll—Part 3.

(4) Instructors form the company in eight files facing the sawdust square from the southwest edge. Let the candidates alternately run and front-roll all the way across the pit, reforming on the other side. Take it slow at first. Come back the same way faster (front roll). Then do the shoulder roll left side going over and right side coming back. Then the "back roll" over and "optional" back.

c. **Falls.**—Assemble again and instructor gives them this information and demonstration: Now often times a person can't roll because there isn't room or because if he were thrown by an opponent, the man he was grappling with would have hold of him. For example, if I put a hip throw on this man he should be able to fall on the deck so as not to injure himself. **Demonstrate.**

(1) **Side Fall.**—See Figure 22.

Now notice how he fell on his side. He kept his head raised high off the deck, his free arm was outflung catching some of his weight, and he twisted his hips, crossing his leg over and catching a goodly portion of his weight on his foot. He didn't land on any parts of his body that would be injured easily. He can fall on either side in this manner. A man can practice falling from the sqatting position. **Demonstrate.**

(2) **Backward Fall.**—Figures 23a, 23b.

When a person falls to the rear he can prevent smashing his head or back by tucking his chin on his chest, arching his body and landing on his outflung arms and his feet like this. Demonstrate falling to rear a couple of times from squatting position. Candidates then turn to and practice these falls from squatting position for three to four minutes. Then assemble again.

Figure 22.—Side Fall.

Figure 23(a).—Back Fall—Part 1.

Figure 23(b).—Back Fall—Part 2.

d. **Footwork.**—Now you have all played some kind of sports at some time or other and you know how important "keeping your eye on the ball" is. But what's another thing that is vital for all sports?—That's right, footwork. And that is just as important in hand-to-hand fighting and bayonet work as it is in sports. A man must be relaxed yet poised at all times, balanced and ready to react instantly in any direction. Throughout our course we will try to train you in improving your footwork.

(1) **Stance.**—The stance we recommend is the so-called boxer's stance with the body faced roughly half right, the arms slightly raised to a ready position, knees slightly bent, feet comfortably apart, left foot forward, toe pointing roughly toward your opponent; right foot back, toe pointing towards the right. The weight is easily balanced between the feet—most of the weight on the balls of the feet. Demonstrate.

(2) **Moving.**—When moving in any direction we use a movement quite similar to the boxer's shuffle moving one foot at a time always relaxed and balanced. It is wise to raise the feet slightly above the ground when moving, however, instead of dragging them. Out in the field there may be roots, stubs, rocks, and the like which could trip you. Now turn to and practice this stance and footwork for a bit and then pair off and shadow box. Candidates turn to and practice stance, footwork, and shadow boxing.

13. 3d Hour of Combat Conditioning; 1st Hour of Judo.

(Instructor's Note.—The company will turn to for a workout by platoons, platoon instructors in charge: Abdominal Rise Rail; 2d Platoon in sawdust square rolls, falls, and Crab Drill; 3d Platoon on obstacle course. Platoons spend 5 minutes on each phase then rotate. Total time about 15 minutes.)

a. **Crab Drill.**—Crab Drill is a mass exercise intended to help the individual's balance, coordination, and physical prowess.

(1) **Face Down Position.**—See Figure 24a.

Face down, hands and feet outstretched to front and rear respectively and spread apart about eighteen (18) inches; body somewhat arched and about one (1) foot off the deck. See Figure 24b.

(2) **Face Up Position.**—Face up and back down; body arched resting on feet and hands as before.

(3) **Movements.**—The body is moved forward, laterally or to the rear in accordance with the platoon instructor's commands. Movements are made by shuffling quickly on "all fours" but keeping the hands and feet within the same general area. Each movement will be made continuously in the direction indicated until otherwise commanded.

R.D. 4443

Figure 24(a).—Crab Drill—Part 1.

Figure 24(b).—Crab Drill—Part 2.

(4) **Commands.**—The platoon instructor's commands are: "Front"; "Rear"; "Left"; "Right"; "Face Down"; and "Face Up". The movements made will correspond. To face "up" or "down" whirl the body around to the new position without lowering the body to the deck.

b. **Abdominal Rises.**—One platoon at the rail at a time. Men paired off; one man sitting with buttocks on the rail, legs horizontal, hands clasped behind head; other man standing in front of him holding first man's ankles under his armpits. Do ten (10) bends and rises on rail to count of platoon instructor. Then change over. If time permits each should do ten more rises to count.

To make the exercise progressively more strenuous, all that is necessary is to keep the arms extended straight overhead and to increase the number of rises made.

Assemble in sawdust square for introductory Judo instruction.

c. **Introduction to Judo.**—(1) By Combat Conditioning Section instructor: This will be your first hour of eight in Judo and disarming in Officer Candidates School. Many of you have learned a lot of the techniques in V-12 training, at boot camp or in the field. For these men it will be a good review and a chance to become more adept and confident in Judo and disarming. To those to whom it will be completely new, we intend to teach several useful moves that can be learned readily by average Marines in a relatively short time. Four hours will be devoted to maiming, takedowns, come-alongs, strangles, and breaks, and four hours to the use of the club, knife, pistol, and garrote and to disarming. We will not stress counters as such, because the way the course is arranged we do not feel it is necessary. You will learn how to react instinctively and in an effective way under any circumstances. Just remember that practice makes perfect and successful hand-to-hand fighting requires a lot of both.

(2) **History.**—The system of unarmed fighting that we Marines study today is supposed to have originated with the ancient Chinese monks who were very often molested by armed bandits from the hills. Since their creed prevented their carrying or using deadly weapons, they devised a system of disarming as a means of self-protection which enabled them, bare-handed, to disarm and overcome an attacker armed with a gun, knife, club or sword. Through many years of use and development the disarming system came to include unarmed hand-to-hand fighting and was studied not only as a defense but also as a sport.

(3) The system of unarmed combat was introduced to the Japanese who developed it further. It was a particularly valuable system because, using it, a person could overcome an opponent who had the advantage of weapons, size or strength. The Japanese called the system "Jiu-Jitsu" which is supposed to mean "to conquer by yielding". The theory of the system was to yield at first to an opponent's attack, then to unbalance him and attack his weakest points in order to overcome him, and in so doing to make the best use of all your own natural weapons. Thus the system stresses taking advantage of an opponent's weight and momentum and of his weak spots such as nerve centers, joints, and vital organs. You can see that a knowledge of anatomy was prerequisite. Also the individual employing Jiu-Jitsu used his fingers, hands, legs, and feet to the fullest advantage at all times thus beating his opponent in the "easy way". Incidentally the select wealthy and the militarists of Japan who studied Jiu-Jitsu applied its philosophy to their everyday lives, striving to overcome their problems both major and minor, the "easy way" and utilizing all their abilities to the fullest advantage.

(4) In about 1830 a certain Professor Jiguro Kano, of the High Normal School of Tokio, improved and standardized Jiu-Jitsu moves and taught them to the police, the army and those others who had the interest and the pecuniary means. The school was called "Judo" meaning "school of learning" and eventually this particular system of combat acquired the name "Judo". As was said before Judo was studied both as a defense and as a sport although it was not

exactly a sport as we know them, for there were no compunctions at hitting below the belt or maiming an opponent. In professional Judo bouts a fighter wishing to save life or limb could acknowledge defeat by rapping the deck with his hand or foot.

(5)   About twenty-five years ago Judo was introduced to the United States. Some interested Americans experimented with the system and adopted it as a sport. They did away with the actual maiming and also developed counters to all of the moves. Judo has been taught for some years at the U. S. Military and Naval Academies. The Marine Corps has adopted Judo only recently and advocates only the simplest and most effective and easily learned movements.

d.   **Judo—Dirty Fighting.**—(1)   Actually the Marine Corps' Judo system amounts to little more than scientific dirty fighting. You have been told this before and we'll tell it to you again now. When it's a question of your life or your opponent's **don't hesitate a fraction of a second—hit him in a vital spot and hit him hard—use all of the natural weapons God gave you and in the most effective manner that you possibly can until you have destroyed him!** That may sound "dirty" and we intend that it should. There is no place for so-called "sportsmanship" in this war. If you don't overcome your enemy with a knee in the crotch first, he'll take advantage of you and kill you. And never forget this, men—when your enemy is fighting for his life he will possess almost superhuman strength. Remember that, and hit him first and hard! Remember too, that if you have fairly strong arms and legs and know how to fight "dirty", that's just about all you will ever need if you are in hand-to-hand combat.

(2)   **Natural Weapons Available.**—Whether a man is up against an armed opponent or an unarmed one, when he is fighting for his life he must use all the natural weapons God gave him: (demonstrate) his fists, hands on edge or open, fingers, elbows, and forearms, knees, feet, and even his teeth. You can even use your head or shoulders to butt with. (Demonstrate the types of blows recommended.) A very hard, sharp, back-hand blow can be delivered with the fleshy part of the hand on edge, just below the little finger's knuckle.

(3)   **The Vital Spots of the Human Body.**—There are a few simple exposed spots of the human body which if hit hard will kill a man. The ones we want you to know and remember are these: (Demonstrate them on an instructor or candidate.)

(4)   **The Throat.**—(See Figures 25a, 25b).   A blow here by edge of hand, fist, or elbow will stun a man; if the blow is hard enough, it will kill him by collapsing his wind-pipe.

R.D. 4443

Figure 25(a).—Dirty Fighting—Throat—Part 1.

R.D. 4443

Figure 25(b).—Dirty Fighting—Throat—Part 2.

(5) **The Back of Neck.**—(See Figure 26). The so-called "rabbit punch" on the back of the neck delivered by hand, fist or foot will either stun a man or kill him by snapping his spine at the neck.

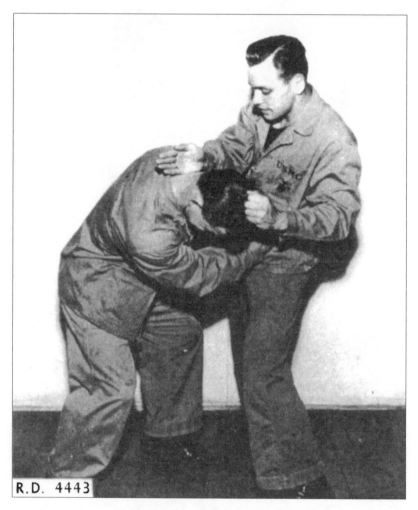

R.D. 4443

Figure 26.—Back of Neck.

R.D. 4443

Figure 27(a).—Solar-Plexus—Part 1.

Figure 27(b).—Solar-Plexus—**Part 2**.

(6) **The Solar-Plexus.**—(See Figures 27a, 27b). A fist or knee here will knock a man out—if hard enough the blow can cause fatal internal injuries.

(7) **Crotch.**—(See Figures 28a, 28b, 28c). This is one of the most vital areas to work on and should always be first in mind. Even a light blow to the testicles will cause great pain. A hard blow to the crotch may cause fatal injuries and is sure to take the fight out of a man in a hurry. Never forget the crotch—hit there automatically! All right, turn to in pairs in platoon areas and point out to each other the most vulnerable areas of the human body and the natural weapons you have available to hit them with.

R.D. 4443

Figure 28(a).—Crotch—Part 1.

Figure 28(b).—Crotch—Part 2.

Figure 28(c).—Crotch—Part 3.

(8) **Assemble again.**—Those are the places we recommend to hit for whenever the opportunity presents itself because they are most vulnerable spots of man. They are exposed and soft enough so that you can do the dirty work without hurting your hands or any other parts of your body. In addition to these there are some other vulnerable spots which if attacked may not result in fatal injury but will cause much pain and so distract an enemy sufficiently to help you overcome him. From Head to Foot these spots are: (Point out on a candidate.)

(9) **The Hair.**—All you have to do is grab as much as you can and tear with all you've got.

(10) **The Ears.**—Can be torn or bitten off. Very painful. Also can be boxed with palm of hand which is a very good temporary distraction. Makes the ears ring.

(11) **The Bridge of Nose.**—(See Figure 29). Best to hit with the cutting edge of the hand. May break the nose and will temporarily blind the man. Is claimed by some experts to be a vital spot.

(12) **The Nostrils.**—Can tear with fingers.

(13) **The Eyes.**—(See Figure 30). Can jab with the fingers or can gouge out with the thumbs. Guaranteed to distract an enemy who has a hold on you.

R.D. 4443

Figure 29.—Bridge of Nose.

Figure 30.—Eyes.

(14) **Upper Lip.**—Another sensitive area vulnerable for a blow with cutting edge of hand.

(15) **The Mouth.**—Can also tear with the fingers.

(16) **The Jaw.**—See Figure 31. A hard blow on the point or side will stun a man.

(17) **The Kidney.**—See Figure 32. A hard blow with knee, fist or edge of hand will stun a man and may cause serious internal injuries. However it is often partially protected by a cartridge belt.

R.D. 4443

Figure 31.—Jaw.

Figure 32.—Kidney.

(18) **The Knee Cap.**—Best attacked with the foot—can be very painfully hurt by a good blow of toe or heel.

(19) **The Back of Leg.**—See Figure 33. Good to kick just back of knee. Painful and helpful in forcing a man down.

(20) **The Shins.**—See Figure 34. Good to kick with toe or heel or to scrape with sole.

R.D. 4443

Figure 33.—Back of Knee and Leg.

Figure 34.—Knee Cap and Shin.

(21) **The Feet and Ankles.**—See Figure 35. Excellent to stamp on. The insteps or arches can be broken fairly easily by such a blow.

(22) We recommend you go for these spots if you and your enemy are already closed in and if the other spots aren't accessible. (From a clinched position demonstrate all of above once more as they may actually be used. Simulate the blows).

Figure 35.—Foot and Ankle.

(23)   In addition to the spots we have just mentioned, there are also the limbs and joints which are weak when forced into abnormal positions. For example, fingers, wrists, and arms may be bent back against the joint causing great pain. The legs can be worked over also. In addition, to attack the inside of the wrists, elbows, or knees with hands or feet is good for distraction or helping break holds.

(24) Now there are more places on the human body than these which can be very effectively worked on but these we have showed you and the few that we will show you later on are enough to know. They are simple, exposed and are easy to find and work on.

(25) Just one more thing before we turn to again. Throughout our entire course, whether it is a Judo throw, a disarming move, or a bayonet stroke that you're executing, we want you to **simulate following through every time in the way we prescribe!** Carry out the complete movement every time, simulating only those parts of it that would actually injure your partner! If you follow through in practice, it will come naturally when you need it the most. **Remember—it isn't enough to throw a man or disarm him in a fight to the death unless you follow through and finish him off!**

(26) Don't forget your stance and footwork. Have your feet spread about shoulder's width; left foot forward, knees flexed; weight on balls of feet evenly; trunk bent forward slightly and eyes to the front; hands before you; ready to react in any direction to any situation which may confront you. Move by shuffling—(demonstrate) don't drag your feet. Now pair off and practice simulating hitting for all vital spots. Use the most effective weapon for the particular vital spot to be hit.

Candidates turn to and practice for about five (5) minutes.

Assemble again for instruction on Takedowns.

e. **Takedowns.**—The first thing we will consider is the variety of ways to take an enemy to the ground. Each one of the ways we will teach you has its advantages and disadvantages—learn to appreciate both and make use of the former. Remember that you must never expect to fall into an ideal situation for a takedown or for any hold for that manner. You must make your own openings and take advantage of them. These movements we will teach you will work if you make them work. It is up to **you** to do that!

(1) **Hip Throw.**—(Demonstrated).

1. Grab opponent's left side with your right hand pushing his side away from you. Grab his right arm underneath the elbow with your left hand, pulling it toward you.

2. Secure his right hand under your left elbow and armpit pressing hard against his elbow (arm straight) and obtaining a lever-like action which will help twist his right shoulder toward you. Simultaneously push his left side (with your right hand) away from you. See Figure 36a.

R.D. 4443

Figure 36(a).—Hip Throw—Part 1.

Figure 36(b).—Hip Throw—Part 2.

3. With your right foot step quickly across the left and behind your opponent's right (still keeping your feet well under you and maintaining balance), bend your knees and get your right hip under your opponent's right hip. Push his weight onto your hip.

4. Straighten up your legs sharply and at the same time bend your trunk forward pulling back on your opponent's right elbow and pushing forward and down on his torso with your right arm. This will spin your opponent off the ground and onto your hip. See Figure 36b.

5. When he is highest in the air suddenly pull out your hip from beneath him and fall hard on top of him to the deck. He will land on his back, head or shoulder blades; you should land with your right shoulder on his chest and right forearm in ribs, stomach or crotch.

6. Follow through instantly with hard blows by knee, fist, or edge of hand to the immediately accessible vital spots.

(2) **Variation of Hip Throw.**—(Demonstrated).

1-2-3-and 4—Same as before.

5. Instead of falling on top of man when he is thrown, bend knees and squat, retaining hold on enemy's right arm so that his right upper arm lands on your left

knee catching the entire force of his fall and breaking his arm. See Figure 36c. It is not even necessary that his arm land on your knee, for if you rest your left forearm on your left knee, the effect will be the same.

6. Follow through with edge of hand blows to the throat and crotch.

R.D. 4443

Figure 36(c).—Variation of Hip Throw—Part 3.

(3) Turn to and practice these two takedowns in platoon areas, company instructors with their respective platoons. In practicing the variation of the hip throw be careful to have your left knee low so as not to injure your partner. Simulate the follow-through blows for both movements, making them a part of the entire movement.

Ten (10) minutes.

(4) **Rear Leg Trip.**—A very quick, simple, and effective takedown. (Demonstrated.)

1. Grab your enemy by the dungarees, preferably his left side with your right hand and his right elbow with your left.

2. Swing your right leg across your left and behind his right leg (note how this movement protects your crotch).

3. Swing your right leg and heel back **sharply,** kicking his right leg (at the knee or just below) out from under him, at the same time pressing him back and down. See Figure 37.

4. Your opponent will go down hard on his back. Stay with him landing hard on top of him and drawing back your right fist.

5. Swing your right fist up hard into his crotch.

Turn to and practice the Rear Leg Trip (simulate crotch blow).

Five (5) minutes.

R.D. 4443

Figure 37.—Rear Leg Trip.

14.   4th Hour of Combat Conditioning—2d Hour of Judo.—
Assemble in sawdust square.

a.   **Takedowns.**—Combat Conditioning instructor: We
will continue working on simple and effective takedowns. First
of all, are there any questions on the Hip Throw and variation
or on the Rear Leg Trip?

(1)   All right, now the rear leg trip can be used
if a man is tugging you toward him. You must act fast to
make it work. Resist his pulling just enough to make him pull
harder, then yield suddenly and put the rear leg trip on him.

(Demonstrate this a couple of times.)

(2)   **Front Leg Trip.**—To be used if an opponent
is crowding you backward.

1.   Try and grasp an elbow and a side with
your hands as in the Rear Leg Trip.

2.   Resist his pushing you backwards just
enough to make him push harder.

3.   Suddenly turn either side to him extending
your leg closest to him (knee slightly bent, foot planted on
deck) and drop down on the knee farthest from him. (Note how
this movement protects your crotch.)   Help his momentum
by pulling him towards you.

4.   Simultaneously twist his body (by pushing
and pulling with your hands) so that his side is turned to
you (this follows naturally with your own turning—his right
side come to yours or vice versa) and pull him across your
extended leg causing him to land on his side or back. You
land hard on top of him.

5.   Follow up instantly by hard blows to the
throat and crotch.

(3)   **Alternate Front Leg Trip.**—(Demonstrated.)

1.   Same.—But catch opponent's right arm
with your left as in the Hip Throw.

2.   Same.

3.   Same—But turn your **right** side to him.

4.   Same except don't land on top of him, but
pull up sharply with both hands underneath his right elbow
(still keeping his right hand trapped under your armpit) just
before he lands, thus breaking his arm. (Simulate the "hard"
part in practice.)

5.   Same.

Emphasize that quickness and balance are important in
both of these takedowns. Turn to in platoon areas and practice
(6 minutes).

Assemble again and take up Drop Kick takedown.

(4)   **Drop Kick.**—Good if worked fast before your
opponent closes in too much. (Demonstrated.)

1. Reach forward with both hands and grab hold of enemy's coat by the lapels, collar, or breast and at the same time raise up your right (left if preferred) foot and plant it hard in his crotch (in practice place foot gently in stomach). The wrists can be crossed (optional) when you grab the lapels—for some people it is easier this way and a more effective strangle can be worked from it. See Figure 38a.

Figure 38(a).—Drop Kick—Part 1.

2. Throw back your head, pull your opponent towards you and sit down fast, not bending your right leg too much. This will start to throw your opponent over your head. You will be rolling on your back on the deck. See Figure 38b.

3. Straighten out your leg sharply, throwing your opponent clear over you. **Be sure and retain your original grasp on his coat firmly! Never let go your grip!**

4. Before he lands flat on his back, roll over onto your knees and elbows and draw his coat tightly across his throat scissorlike, cutting off his wind. The combination of the kick in crotch, slam to the deck, and pressure on windpipe should overcome the enemy in a hurry. See Figure 38c.

Practice in platoon areas for five (5) minutes.

Figure 38(b).—Drop Kick—Part 2.

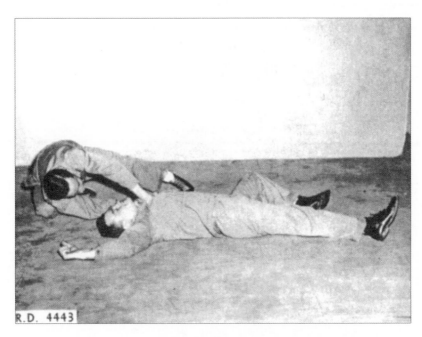

Figure 38(c).—Drop Kick—Part 3.

Assemble for work with belt pull.

(5) **Belt Pull.**—A very effective takedown that should leave the man beaten by the time he hits the deck with you on top. (Demonstrated.)

1. With right fist punch adversary hard in the stomach.

2. With right hand grab hold of his belt or if none his clothing and pull him towards you.

3. At the same time bring the heel of your left hand up hard under his chin bending his head way back and gouging his eyes with your fingers and simultaneously knee him hard in the crotch with your right knee. See Figure 39. The combination of the belt pull, blow on jaw, bent-back neck, and knee in crotch will drop the man. Go down with him.

4. As you go down on top of him turn your right side into your man (thus protecting your own crotch) and land with all your weight on your knee in his crotch.

Practice the Belt Pull for about (5) minutes, simulating wherever necessary. Assemble again for a variation.

Figure 39.—Belt Pull.

(6)　Variation of the Belt Pull—**The Body Pickup.**
(Demonstrated.) 1 and 2 same as for Belt Pull.

3.　Swing a hard blow to his throat or jaw
with your left forearm (arm tightly flexed) putting plenty of
shoulder into the blow.

4.　Leaving your left forearm right where it
is, grab hold of his collar or lapel with your left hand.

5.　Simultaneously with (4) step to his right
side with your left foot, at the same time swinging your right
hand vigorously up underneath his crotch (delivering a blow
with your arm as you do) and grabbing hold of his belt, trous-
ers or coat at the rear. See Figure 40a.

6. Pick the man up; then drop him head first to the deck, holding onto his right thigh with your right arm.

7. If he falls just right on his head, it may break his neck. Maintain your grip around his right thigh and keep your right knee in the small of his back to balance him on his neck. See Figure 40b. Drop down onto his face with your left knee. Pummel his face, throat, and crotch with your left hand.

Figure 40(a).—Body Pickup—Part 1.

Figure 40(b).—Body Pickup—Part 2.

(7) **Alternative to Body Pickup.**—(Demonstrated.)
1, 2, 3, 4, 5—Same.

6. Same—Except drop the man hard on your right knee (contacting his spine at small of back) breaking his back.

(8) **The Football Tackle.**—Familiar to all—keep eyes on opponent; dive for legs; hit thighs with shoulder anywhere from knees up; wrap arms tightly around legs; drive opponent down landing hard on top. Turn to and practice these last three moves for about eight (8) minutes.

Assemble again and then call upon candidate volunteers to demonstrate all the takedowns covered in the two hours. Answer any pertinent questions.

15. 5th Hour of Combat Conditioning—3d Hour of Judo.

a. Workout.

1st Platoon—Abdominal Rise Rail.

2d Platoon—Sawdust pit: Roll across pit; duckwalk back; roll across again; then pushups controlled by platoon instructors.

3d Platoon—Obstacle Course.

(1) Allow five (5) minutes for each phase and then rotate etc. Total time 15-20 minutes. Then assemble in pit. Combat Conditioning Section instructor: You men have learned a lot from the first two hours of Judo if you know what vital spots to hit and how to hit them. In addition if you can execute well one good takedown and can follow through automatically and effectively you're just about set. There isn't much more that you really need to learn. Just remember though that practice makes perfect and that you should be able to react automatically in any situation. That is why we have a few more basic moves for various situations we want to teach you. First of all the Strangle. The Strangle is an essential part of hand-to-hand fighting and has been used in this war.

b. **Japanese Strangle.**—The most effective simple strangle we know. It can be used to take a man down quite noiselessly from the rear. Like all other holds a good deal depends upon the element of surprise and how the other man reacts. (Demonstrated.)

1. Approach enemy quietly from the rear to secure element of surprise. Have your right forearm ready to slip around his throat and your left arm forward, forearm vertical.

2. From the right, slip your right forearm hard against enemy's windpipe catching hold of clothing inside of left elbow with fingers of right hand. See Figure 41a.

3. Instantly bring the palm of the left hand to bear hard against the back of his head and pull your elbows towards you. Knee him hard in the small of his back or kick the back of his knee. Pull his head way back with your arms, setting him down to the deck and continue the strangle from there. See Figure 41b. Notice how the neck is caught in a "scissors" by this action. The pressure on the back of the head forces the neck forward and the act of bringing back the elbows forces the forearm into the windpipe.

As an alternative the strangle can be applied in a slightly different manner which, if done vigorously, will snap the spine at the neck. The difference is simply that the throat is caught in the crook of the right elbow and the right hand is brought way back past the enemy's left shoulder, while the left hand goes against the **right rear** of the enemy's head and forces his head sharply forward and to the left.

R.D. 4443

Figure 41(a).—Japanese Strangle—Part 1.

Figure 41(b).—Japanese Strangle—Part 2.

c. **Strangle Breaks.**—The first reaction you should have at feeling hands or arms at your throat is to "bull" your neck (i.e.—tuck your chin in hard and swell your neck muscles), duck down sharply by bending your knees and your body forward from the waist and strike a blow for your assailant's crotch with elbow, edge of hand, fist or knee. As we said before, success in strangles as in all holds depends a lot upon surprise, quickness, and reaction. Reacting instantly against a strangle as we have just described should break most strangles. There are specific breaks we recommend that you learn for the type of strangles you might expect in case your instinctive reaction moves of "bulling" neck, ducking and hitting for crotch don't succeed in breaking the strangle.

(1) **Escapes from Japanese Strangle.**—In order of preference. (Demonstrated.)

(a) **Crotch Blow.**—1. Bull neck and bend knees sharply.

2. With right hand grasp opponent's right trouser leg pulling it to right and at same time moving your right knee to left and turning your body to the right.

3. With right hand or elbow hit hard for his crotch.

4. Follow through in the best manner possible.

(b) **Trip.**—1. Same.

2. Step behind your opponent's left leg with your right.

3. With your right arm across the front of his body sweep him backwards, tripping him over your right leg, and, twisting yourself strongly towards him (clockwise), fall on top of him.

4. Strike hard with your left fist for his crotch.

(c) **Work on Fingers.**—(Assume that he has his **right** arm against your throat. Reverse procedure for **left** arm. Break is ineffective if opponent's fingers are not exposed.)

1. Raise both arms high and well back of his elbows, groping with both hands for your opponent's fingers of left hand which are pressing on the back of your head. Figure 42a.

2. Secure any number of fingers with either hand and bend them back against the joints thus tearing his hand away from the back of your head. Catch the crook of his left arm well up inside your left elbow and retain it there.

3. Transfer the finger(s) you are bending back to your left hand (if not already there) assisting the pressure with the right hand and keeping his left elbow trapped inside your own. Figure 42b.

4. Simultaneously with 2. or 3. force his fingers and hand back past his shoulder and down. He will experience extreme pain in the fingers, wrist, and shoulder and will go down rapidly. Kick him in the face as he goes.

5. Follow through with hard blows to the throat and crotch. See Figure 42c.

Turn to and practice all four breaks from the Japanese strangle. (10 minutes.)

R.D. 4443

Figure 42(a).—Break from Jap Strangle—Part 1.

Figure 42(b).—Break from Jap Strangle—Part 2.

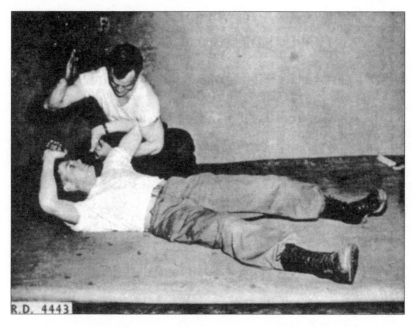

Figure 42(c).—Break from Jap Strangle—Part 3.

16. 6th Hour of Combat Conditioning—4th Hour of Judo.—
Assemble in area south of sawdust square for demonstration of Break from Forearm Strangle.

a. **Strangle Breaks—Breaks from Forearm Strangle in Order of Preference.—**(1) Same as first method for Japanese Strangle Break, that is, "bull" neck, duck, grab trouser leg, and hit for crotch. Follow through.

(2) Same as second method for Japanese Strangle Break, that is, "bull" neck, duck, and leg trip. Follow through.

(3) **Flying Mare.—**(a) "Bull" neck, duck down, bending knees sharply.

(b) Reach up with hands grabbing his arms.

(c) Pull him over you and at the same time straighten your knees out throwing him over your head to the deck.

(d) Follow through quickly with blows to the throat, face, and crotch.

This move cannot be worked if your opponent already has a strong knee in your back or a foot kicking the back of your knee.

(4) **Hammer Lock.—**(Assume enemy's lower arm about your neck is his **right**—reverse procedure for **left**).

   (a) "Bull" neck and duck down, bending knees sharply.

   (b) With your left hand pull down hard on his lower wrist and push up sharply with your right hand on his lower elbow (Figure 43a) at the same time ducking your head out from under his arm and stepping to his right rear retaining your hold with both hands on his arm. See Figure 43b.

   (c) Work his right arm into a hammer lock by bending his arm and forcing his hand up between his shoulder blades. While you are doing this, work your left forearm up under his forearm and place your left hand on his right shoulder, thus securing the hammerlock and setting your right hand free.

   (d) Using the hammer lock, force your opponent down kneeing him in the face with your right knee and delivering a hard "rabbit punch" with the cutting edge of your right hand.

  Turn to in sawdust pit and practice the four breaks for the Forearm Strangle (10 minutes), then assemble for Front Hand Strangle Breaks.

R.D. 4443

Figure 43(a).—Break from Forearm Strangle—Hammer Lock—Part 1.

Figure 43(b).—Break from Forearm Strangle—Hammer Lock—Part 2.

b. **Strangle Breaks—Breaks from Front Hand Strangle in Order of Preference.**—(1) **Hand Wedge.**—(a) "Bull" neck and duck low by bending knees; clasp hands tightly.

(b) Bring hands and arms in a wedge straight up sharply, knocking away your opponent's hands.

(c) Bring the cutting edges of your hands still clasped tightly down hard on the bridge of your opponent's nose.

(d) Swing the clasped hands up into his crotch.

(2) **Wrist Throws.**—Working on same **Hand and Wrist.**

(a) Bring your right hand across to his right hand at your throat striking his left forearm with your arm as you do, to help loosen his grip. If your opponent is shorter than you, swing your right over his left arm, if taller swing under.

(b) Lay the palm of your right hand across the back of his right, grasping firmly the cutting edge of his hand with your fingers. You may or may not press your thumb on the back of his hand near forefinger knuckles. Figure 44a.

(c) In one movement swing your shoulders around to the right, (dropping your right shoulder and raising your left as you do), come up hard with the palm of your left hand underneath his right elbow, and tear his right hand from your throat bending his wrist way back (palm towards wrist) with your right hand. Figure 44b.

(d) Force your opponent down to the deck applying the "bar" (lever) forcefully all the way (i.e., elbow straight and wrist bent way back). Prevent his rolling out of it by blocking his back with your right knee. Kick him in the face with your left foot or drop down on his face or side with your left knee and pummel his face, throat, and crotch with your left hand.

R.D. 4443

Figure 44(a).—Wrist Throw—Same Hand Wrist—Part 1.

Figure 44(b).—Wrist Throw—Same Hand Wrist—Part 2.

(3) **Working on Opposite Hand and Wrist.—**
(a) Same as in (2) and at the same time place palm of your **left** hand across the back of his right hand, grasping his hand between the forefinger and thumb. Press your thumb on knuckle of small finger to get added leverage. Figure 44c.

(b) As one movement swing your shoulders to the left (dropping your left shoulder and raising your right as you do), strike down hard with your right hand on edge inside of his right elbow helping to break his grip, and tear his hand back (palm towards wrist) and forcing it past his right shoulder. Figure 44d.

(c)   Assist your left hand by grasping his right hand with yours, fingers inside his palm and thumb on the back of his hand bearing back hard. If your opponent has a very strong arm then with your right arm reach underneath his right upper arm and place your hand on the back of his right hand, forcing his hand back down past his shoulder in a lever-like action.

(d)   As he goes down kick or knee him in the crotch or use your left knee in his head. Figure 44e.

NOTE: In all moves where a man is brought under control by strain on wrist joints, it should be emphasized that the force is applied to the **hand**—not the wrist.

Turn to—practice break from Front Strangle (10 minutes).

Figure 44(c).—Wrist Throw—Same Hand Wrist—Part 3.

Figure 44(d).—Wrist Throw—Same Hand Wrist—Part 4.

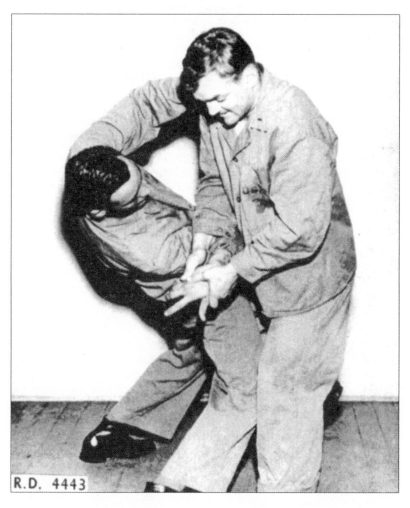

Figure 44(e).—Wrist Throw—Same Hand Wrist—Part 5.

Assemble for demonstration of Breaks from Bear Hugs.

c. **Break for Bear Hug from Front—Hit for Vital Spot.**

d. **Break for Bear Hug around Waist or Chest from the Rear.**

NOTE: This is a rather ineffective hold in itself and easily broken.

(1) **The Flying Mare.**—(a) Bend knees fast ducking down, throwing his weight onto your back.

(b) Reach up with hands, grab his head and throw him over your head by straightening your knees and pulling down on his head.

(2) **Alternative—The Body Pick-Up**—(a) Bend the knees and step to the left and rear with the left foot, at the same time reaching over and grasping his right trouser leg and the knee with your right hand. See Figure 45a.

(b) Step quickly behind him with your right foot, staying on balance and grasp his left knee with your left hand. Figure 45b.

(c) Pick the man up in your arms, let go with your right hand and ram your right elbow into the bridge of his nose. If he still has the bear hug on you it is working toward his swift downfall because with his arms engaged around you, you are unopposed in battering his face and throat with your elbow or edge of hand. Figure 45c. This movement can also be used as a break for a strangle from the rear.

R.D. 4443

Figure 45(a)—Bear Hug, Arms Free—Body Pickup—Part 1.

Figure 45(b).—Bear Hug, Arms Free—Body Pickup—Part 2.

Figure 45(c).—Bear Hug, Arms Free—Body Pickup—Part 3.

(3) **Arms Trapped.**—(a) Duck fast by bending knees sharply and at same time raising elbows high up to sides breaking his hold. As you do this, twist your body towards your opponent.

(b) Hammer your elbow into your opponent's crotch.

Instructor's Note: Turn to and practice these three moves for 5 minutes. If there is any time left assemble and take up a few less important breaks for the Bear Hug from rear.

(4) **Arms Free.**—The Switch—a well-known wrestling move.

113

(a)   Swing your right arm (palm out) around to the right over his right elbow.

(b)   Step to the right with your right foot, turning your body to the right and catch your hand in his crotch, bearing the palm against the inside of his right thigh.

(c)   Pivoting on the ball of your right foot, turn your body all the way to the right, stepping around with your left foot. The pressure on his elbow combined with your whirl to the right about will force him to lose his grip on you and will place you behind him.

(d)   Pull him backwards and kick the back of his knees hard, taking him down to the deck and landing on him with your left knee or elbow.

(e)   Follow up by blows to the throat, bridge of nose, solar-plexus, and crotch.

(5)   **Wrist Lock.**—Good only if your opponent has a hand exposed. Won't work if his fingers are interlocked. (Assume that his **right** hand is "free"—reverse procedure for **left**.)

(a)   Expedite the break by stamping on his feet—clamp your right arm above his right elbow, lay your left palm across his right hand, grasp the cutting edge of his hand with your fingers, and twist and push his right hand vigorously back, bending his palm toward the wrist.

(b)   Grasp your left wrist with your right hand thus securing the wrist back on his left arm. Be sure and keep his left elbow inside your own. See Figure 46a. Wheel around to your left as you do, forcing him down to the deck. (See Figure 46b). You can transfer your right hand to his right upper arm to maintain the leverage. Keep his elbow straight at all times.

(c)   Kick him in the face and body and continue bearing down with the wrist lock. Be sure to simulate the maiming action in practice. (See Figure 46c.)

R.D. 4443

Figure 46(a).—Bear Hug, Arms Free—Wrist Lock—Part 1.

Figure 46(b).—Bear Hug, Arms Free—Wrist Lock—Part 2.

Figure 46(c).—Bear Hug, Arms Free—Wrist Lock—Part 3.

(6) **Arms Trapped—Leg Trip.**—Crowd back on your opponent, reach back with a leg and trip him, falling back on top of him. Turn into him as you fall and work a knee or elbow into his crotch or stomach.

Practice these for 5 minutes.

Instructor's Note: If there is still time left assemble the company for demonstration of Muscle Strumming.

e. **Muscle Strumming.**—A system of working on the nerves in certain fairly accessible muscles to expedite breaking of holds.

Muscle Strumming is entirely secondary in close-in fighting. It is recommended for use in clinched fighting with an opponent when no vital spots are accessible—and then only.

(1)　For Example.—(Demonstrate.)

When caught in a bear hug from the front you can dig your thumbs deep under the large muscles at junction of neck and shoulder (trapezius muscle) and, squeezing down on top with your fingers, massage the muscles vigorously. Figure 47a.

(2)　Other muscles besides the **trapezius** which can be strummed effectively from a clinched position are the chest muscles and the back muscles.

(3)　Grab the chest muscles **(pectoralis, major)** from the front, digging your first two fingers way up underneath and close to the ribs and pressing down with the thumbs, massaging and pinching the muscle vigorously. Seee Figure 47b.

(4)　Grab the large back muscle along either side just below opponent's armpits. (Latissimus Dorsi.) Dig thumbs well underneath close to the ribs. Pinch and strum. See Figure 47c.

(5)　Hook your index fingers over your opponent's collar bones (clavicles) and dig them down deep behind. This can be quite painful to him if done vigorously. Figure 47d.

The Japanese are in general a small-muscled people although there are Japs who are stocky and well-muscled. Muscle Strumming is most effective on small muscles. Often it won't work on a large-muscled person because the important nerves are too well-covered by muscle. Muscle Strumming also requires a strong grip. Naturally Muscle Strumming will not work if there are many clothes in the way. In the Southwest Pacific the chances are that you won't be wearing any heavy clothes.

Turn to and practice Muscle Strumming (5 minutes).

R.D. 4443

Figure 47(a).—Muscle Strumming—Part 1.

R.D. 4443

Figure 47(b).—Muscle Strumming—Part 2.

Figure 47(c).—Muscle Strumming—Part 3.

Figure 47(d).—Muscle Strumming—Part 4.

(6) Note for instructors: If time permits, assemble again and let candidates demonstrate what they have learned about strangles and breaks. The most vital movements are covered early in the hours and the less important moves afterwards as time permits.

(7) A few "come-alongs" can be included for interest's sake if time still permits. Point out that these would never be used on the enemy but are effective for brawls, quieting drunks, etc. They all depend upon quickness, ideal position and surprise for their effectiveness.

f. **Come-Alongs.** — (1) **Thumb-Catch Come-Along.**— Position—facing opponent.

122

(a) Move your left hand forward palm up. Catch your opponent's right thumb between your thumb and forefinger. See Figure 48a.

(b) At the same time catch his right sleeve at the elbow with your right hand and pull it towards you, force his right hand up towards his armpit, bending his arm and bending his wrist back (palm of hand to wrist). Figure 48b.

(c) Secure the crook of his right elbow well within the crook of your left elbow and bear down hard with your left hand on the back of his right hand, completing the come-along. Figure 48c.

R.D. 4443

Figure 48(a).—Thumb Catch—Come Along—Part 1.

Figure 48(b).—Thumb Catch—Come Along—Part 2.

Figure 48(c).—Thumb Catch—Come Along—Part 3.

(2) **Hand-Shake Come-Along.**—Position facing opponent.

(a) Grasp his right hand in yours as in a handshake.

(b) Suddenly pull him towards you and at the same time step to his right with your left foot so that you are more or less side to side—his right to your left. Figure 49a.

(c) Reach under his arm and come down sharply with the cutting edge of your left hand on the inside of his right elbow. At the same time bend the back of his hand toward his wrist helping to bend the arm also. Figure 49b.

(d)   Secure the crook of his right elbow well within the crook of your left elbow and bear down hard with your left hand on the palm of his hand, thus securing the Come-Along.   Figure 49c.

R.D. 4443

Figure 49(a).—Hand Shake—Come Along—Part 1.

R.D. 4443

Figure 49(b).—Hand Shake—Come Along—Part 2.

Figure 49(c).—Hand Shake—Come Along—Part 3.

(3) **Simple Hand Trick that Will Force an Opponent Quickly to His Knees.**

Position: Side by side. Works either way. Consider your left to his right.

(a) Slip your left hand, palm towards you inside of his right hand (palm to palm) and grasp the hand from the rear.

(b) Bring your left elbow up and on top of his forearm and bear straight down, dropping your body straight down.

SECTION 4

PISTOL, SILENT WEAPONS, AND CLUB

17. Seventh Hour.—Company assembled in a circle. Half of company equipped with drawn wooden pistols and the other half with wooden clubs.

18. The Pistol, General.—a. Combat Conditioning Section Instructor: This hour we will start off by devoting a short time to the use of the pistol, pistol disarming and searching prisoners. This is probably not as important as other parts of our course but we feel it deserves some time. Although the pistol has been discontinued as on organic weapon of Marine Corps line units, there are still quite a lot of pistols in use today in the Corps, and both the German and the Japanese enemy employ them extensively.

b. If you should have occasion to use a pistol in the field you probably will want to know enough about it to shoot it fairly effectively. You may have occasion to actually take an enemy prisoner in the field and you should know how to do it with a pistol as well as with some other weapon. There's not much to it anyway. Here is what to do and what not to do. (Demonstrate.) Just keep the pistol close to your side and out of reach of your prisoner's hands or feet. Keep your other hand in a position of readiness to ward off any move the prisoner may make to disarm you. (See Figure 50.) This presumes that your prisoner is valuable to you alive and not as a corpse and that he is aware of that fact. Never place a pistol against an enemy's stomach or back because it will give him a fighting chance of disarming you, especially if you are a little off guard, and not too "trigger-happy". Make the prisoner keep his hands up high. Many Japs speak English which will help you get your idea across. You can always make signs too.

Figure 50.—Pistol—Taking a Prisoner.

19. Searching of Prisoners Using the Pistol.—a. The pistol is an excellent weapon to have if you are alone and are about to search one or more prisoners. You have several alternatives, but there are just two that we recommend. The first is the simplest and the best. Your first worry is about concealed weapons, and since they are frequently carried in the clothes you can make the prisoner strip off all his clothes and then move away while you search them. If you're alone and there is more than one to be searched, have them disrobe one at a time. Those who are not stripping will stand back, with their hands raised. Be sure they strip off **all** their clothing. Japs have been known to carry concealed weapons even in their G-strings, although this is not a common practice.

b. The second method of searching for concealed weapons is to force the prisoner or prisoners to lean against trees or a wall if available. If there's no wall, make them kneel on the deck with all their weight supported by their toes and knuckles. If they are leaning against a vertical surface have their arms extended and legs well to the rear so that the body approximates an angle of 45° with the horizontal. If they are on the deck, then make sure that the body is arched and arms and legs are well extended to front and rear respectively.

c. Having got the prisoner into position, you now proceed to search him. You will search first one side for weapons and then the other. Let's say we start from the prisoner's right side. Come up to his right rear and hook your left toe inside his right foot so that if he makes a false move you can pull the prop out from under him and he'll go down. (Demonstrate.) Stay as far as possible away from him. Hold the pistol up close to your right hip, reach across his body with your left hand, and search his entire left side. Notice that your pistol is out of his reach and also that if you had to fire, your hand would be out of the way. (See Figure 51.) Just remember when you search one side of him, you do it with your hand corresponding, but stand on the opposite side and hold the pistol in the opposite hand.

R.D. 4443

Figure 51.—Searching a Prisoner.

d. To search his right side then, all you have to do is change hands with the pistol and search his right side with your right hand from the left rear. (Demonstrate.) To search two men have them down side by side. Search each man's "outboard" side first and then move one of them over to his partner's opposite side and search the "outboard" sides again. In this manner you have searched both men completely without getting yourself between them at all. In similar manner three or more men can be searched simply by lining them up in a row searching the outboard sides of the end men and "leap-frogging" the right flank man to the left flank after each searching. For a single man or two or even three men, the second system (leaning position) is probably the fastest and is fairly effective. For searching more than two or three men by yourself and for being absolutely certain that you get all the weapons, use the first (stripping) method. In very cold climates the leaning method would be the more humane, of course.

20. Pistol Disarming.—It is not altogether impossible that you might have occasion to disarm an enemy armed with a pistol who is holding you prisoner. If the man holds the pistol away from you it would be suicide to try to take it away from him. However, if he holds it in your ribs or back you have a fighting chance of taking it away from him. He might be taking you prisoner at night and be careless enough to prod you with the pistol to show that he meant business. He might be alert at first when taking you prisoner but might later relax just enough to allow you to catch him by surprise. That's when you try to disarm him and then only!

a. **Disarming from the Front.**—Assume pistol in opponent's right hand, muzzle placed near your chest or stomach. Your hands raised. See Figure 52a.

(1) **Parrying Left—Hit Crotch.**—1. Pivot the body to left from the hips, at the same time parrying the pistol to your left with your right hand. (Note that even if you miss the parry your body is still out of the line of fire of the pistol.) Grab the pistol and his fingers from the top with your right hand. See Figure 52b.

2. With your left catch hold of the pistol grip from the bottom, enclosing his fingers. See Figure 52c.

3. Close in fast and knee him in the crotch.

4. To tear the pistol from his grasp (in case you don't intend to finish him but want to hold him prisoner) always work the pistol back against his trigger finger. Notice that this also works against the thumb, which is the weakest part of a person's grip.

Figure 52(a).—Disarming from Front, Parry Left—Hit Crotch—Part 1.

Figure 52(b).—Disarming from Front, Parry Left—Hit Crotch—Part 2.

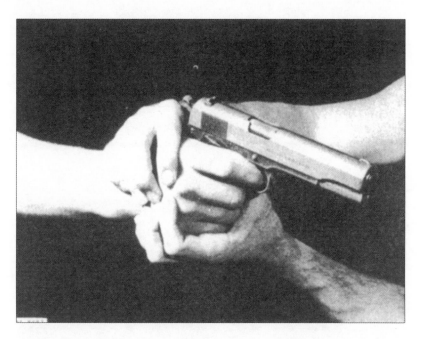

Figure 52(c).—Disarming from Front, Parry Left—Hit Crotch—Part 3.

(2)   Alternate to (1).—**Wrist Throw.**

1, 2—Same.

3.   Still clasping his right hand, and the pistol with both your hands, whirl your hands in a high arc to the right (being sure that the pistol points at him rather than at you as you do) and at the same time step across with your left foot to the right, catch his right upper arm underneath your left armpit, straighten out his right arm, and bend his right hand back hard (palm toward wrist). See Figure 53a. If your grip is strong you can control your enemy with your hands alone thus working the move a trifle faster and keeping him away from you more.

4.   Raise high on his right hand, all the time bending it back hard and at the same time bearing down with your left armpit. This will force him down fast. Kick or knee him in the face. Keep the pistol pointing towards him. See Figure 53b.

R.D. 4443

Figure 53(a).—Disarming from Front, Parry Left—Wrist Throw—
Part 1.

Figure 53(b).—Disarming from Front, Parry Left—Wrist Throw—
Part 2.

(3) **Parrying Right—Hit Crotch.**—1, 2, 3—Same
as in (1) except left and right are reversed.

Alternate to (3)—**Wrist Throw.**

1, 2—Same as in (2)—Wrist Throw, except right and
left are reversed.

3. Swing the pistol and his right hand with
both your hands in an arc to the left at the same time crossing
your right foot over to the left. Bear down hard with your
thumbs on the back of his hand forcing his wrist back (palm
of hand towards wrist) past his right shoulder.

137

4. Continue to force his wrist back, keeping the pistol pointing towards his head. Knee or kick him hard in the crotch. See Figure 54. If he won't go down, use your right foot to work a rear leg trip on him.

Turn to and practice searching prisoners (2d method) and disarming from the front (4 methods). Ten minutes. As semble for demonstration of pistol disarming from rear.

Figure 54.—Disarming from Front, Parry Right—Wrist Throw.

Position.—Back to opponent, hands raised, pistol close to back. Assume pistol held in opponent's right hand. (Can be disarmed with pistol in either left or right hand.) Figure 55a.

b.   **Method for Pistol in Rear Disarming.**—Before trying to execute a disarming move from the rear make sure that it is the **pistol** that is in your back and not a finger, pipestem or stick.

(1)   **Parrying Right.**—1.   Whirl body around to the right, twisting from the hips, stepping around to right with left foot and ducking body down (by bending knees) and at same time bring right arm down and parry the pistol hard to the right with your right elbow. Figure 55b.

2.   Close in rapidly hitting your opponent in the crotch with your right fist and grabbing for the pistol with your left.

3.   Continue to crowd opponent, grabbing the pistol with both hands and kneeing him in the crotch.

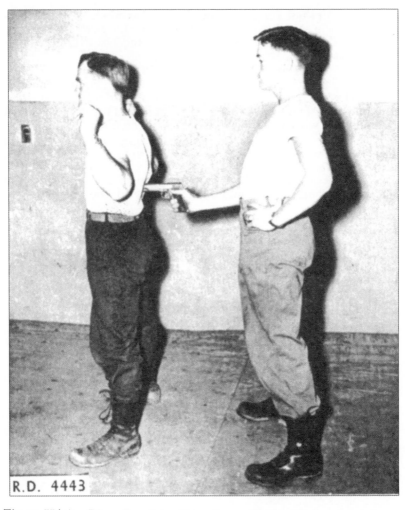

R.D. 4443

Figure 55(a).—Disarming from Rear, Parry Right—Hit Crotch—Part 1.

140

Figure 55(b).—Disarming from Rear, Parry Right—Hit Crotch—Part 2.

(2) **Alternate Method—Wrist Lock.**—1. Same.

2. Bring your right arm underneath and back hard over his right elbow pulling your right hand close to your throat. Figure 56a.

3. Bear down with your right shoulder on his pistol hand forcing the man down. With your left hand push the pistol towards his face. Figure 56b.

4. Knee or kick him in the crotch as he goes down.

R.D. 4443

Figure 56(a).—Disarming from Rear, Parry Right—Wrist Lock—Part 1.

Figure 56(b).—Disarming from Rear, Parry Right—Wrist Lock—Part 2.

(3) **Parrying Left.**—1. Same except whirl to left and parry with your left elbow.

2, 3—Same.

(4) **Alternate Method—Wrist Lock.**—1. Same as (3).

2. Bring your left arm underneath his right arm and back hard over his right elbow pulling your right hand close to your throat.

3. Bear down with your left shoulder forcing the man down. Drive your right knee into his crotch. With your right hand grab the pistol twisting it away from you and towards his head.

4. If the man is considerably taller than you instead of kneeing him in the crotch, Rear Leg Trip him with your right leg behind his and land hard on top of him.

Turn to and practice disarming moves from the rear (4 moves) for about ten minutes.

Assemble for two more disarming moves from the front.

NOTE: These moves should not be tried in an actual disarming situation unless the disarmer is proficient in their use. Nor are they advisable if the man holding the pistol appears to be holding it tensely.

c. **Other Moves.**—(1) **Scissor Break.**—(Assume pistol in opponent's right hand.)

Bring your hands down and across each other sharply in a scissoring motion (hands vertical) so that the cutting edge of your left hand strikes the back of his pistol hand near the knuckles and the cutting edge of your right hand strikes his wrist at the joint. This will knock the pistol completely from his hand. Follow through with a knee in the crotch and a blow across the bridge of his nose.

(2) **Trigger-Finger Break.**—1. With cutting edge of the left hand strike down and to the right on his right wrist (pistol hand) at the same time duck your body to the left.

2. Simultaneously with 1. come upward with right hand (palm down) and catch the pistol barrel in web of your hand (between thumb and forefinger) pushing the muzzle up. Grasp the barrel with your fingers.

3. Without hesitation force the pistol muzzle directly at your opponent (thus breaking his grip and bending back his trigger finger) and bear straight down hard, breaking his trigger finger.

4. Kick opponent in crotch if he has not already shot himself.

Practice these two breaks for about five minutes.

Assemble again. Clear up any questions on the pistol and then demonstrate use of silent weapons.

21. Silent Weapons.—There are some weapons which are particularly adapted for use by scouts on night infiltration work. They are silent and effective and can usually be carried with little or no trouble. These are: The garrote, the machete, the axe, and the blackjack.

a. **The Garrote.**—A silent weapon used to overcome sentries. Consists of about a two-foot length of rather strong and fine wire with wooden handles secured at each end. Hold "normally" in the hands by the handles secured at each end. When approaching a sentry from the rear have wrists crossed, (Figure 57a), drop the loop over his head and draw the wire back tightly, twisting the ends and keeping a continuous pressure on his throat. Figure 57b. A knee in the back assists the

144

takedown. Make it fast so you won't have to try and catch his rifle if he drops it. A strong, fine wire can decapitate a man fairly easily. Barbed wire is to be avoided because of the possibility of the barbs snagging.

R.D. 4443

Figure 57(a).—Garrote—**Taking Down a** Sentry—Part 1.

Figure 57(b).—Garrote—Taking Down a Sentry—Part 2.

b. **The Machete and Axe.**—The machete or the hand axe are often issued by the Quartermaster as part of the individual Marine's field equipment. Pole-axes are sometimes distributed to the troops by engineer personnel for field fortifications work. The machete and the axe are both deadly and are used in the same manner. Approach the enemy from the rear and strike him hard between the shoulder blades with the cutting edge of the weapon. This will probably kill him and even if it doesn't it will hurt him and knock his wind out preventing an outcry. (Demonstrate.)

c. **The Blackjack.**—As you may know or may not know the blackjack can be easily improvised from a G.I. sock, filled with sand, the open end knotted. A blow with it on the side or back of the head is not usually fatal but will usually stun the man, knocking him out and letting you take him prisoner or simply pass by him as you continue on your mission. (Demonstrate.)

22. The Club, General.—a. A good Marine never loses his weapons but there may be a time through no fault of his own a Marine might find himself unarmed in the presence of an enemy. If the unarmed Marine can pick up a club-sized stick it can be a great asset to his fighting effectiveness and chances of coming out alive. With a club he can defend himself against a knife attack and has quite an advantage over an unarmed attacker provided of course that he knows how to use the club. Although in many cases it won't be possible to obtain an ideal sized club it is a good idea for the Marine to learn simple club fighting technique with a club of ideal size. The club should be about 1"-2" in diameter and 2'-2½' in length. It can be held in whichever hand is natural and at either end of the club.

b. **The Long Hold.**—(Demonstrate.)

Grip the club near the end, fairly tightly. The long hold is recommended for defense against knife attack because it gives you more reach than your opponent and is also a natural grip. To defend against knife attack with the long hold on the club hit your opponent in the face, knees, shins, arms, crotch, or throat with the "long" end of the club. Figure 58a. A good knife fighter will not commit his entire weight unless you are down or immobilized and will thrust and slash at any openings he can reach. Keep him at bay and if possible knock the knife from his hands and finish him with your club, taking care that he does not grab it with his free hand. Figure 58b.

Figure 58(a).—Club—Long Hold as in Knife Defense—Part 1.

Figure 58(b).—Club—Long Hold as in Knife Defense—Part 2.

c. **The Short Hold.**—(Demonstrate.)

(1)   Grasp the club near the opposite end so that you have about 6"-8" of club "above" your hand a foot and a half or more "below" your hand. This grip is not a natural one, but it is recommended for fighting against an unarmed man because extra reach is not too important and because it is much more difficult for an enemy to grab the club than it is with the long hold. Some persons find it advantageous to lay their forefingers along the length of the club, pointing towards the short end. The rest of the fingers grip the club.

(2)   An unarmed enemy will try to close in rapidly and also try to wrest the stick away from you. Hold the stick back near your body keeping your free hand advanced to

149

ward off any leads he may make or to grab him if possible and make an opening. When you get an opening almost anywhere on the body strike it with the club either by thrusting hard with the blunt "short" end of the club or by flicking the "long" end of the club out (by a flick of your wrist) and laying it hard across the exposed area. Figure 59a. The latter method of hitting gives you extra reach and is good for punishing the knees, shins, and crotch. The former method (jabbing) is good when you are closing in or already closed in and is good for the stomach, crotch, kidney, ribs, neck, and head. Figure 59b.

R.D. 4443

Figure 59(a).—Club—Short Hold—Part 1.

Figure 59(b).—Club—Short Hold—Part 2.

(3) **A Simple Fighting Sequence.**—A simple sequence of club fighting with the short hold which is recommended for actual fighting as well as to give Marines practice
in handling a club and hitting various types of damaging
blows is done as follows:

     1. With the "short" hold in the right hand
thrust the short end of the club into your opponent's stomach
or scrape it hard with a right hook with the club. See Figure 59b.

     2. Catch hold of the "long" end of the club
with your left hand and swing the club up vertically, "short"
end (right hand) first, scraping the solar-plexus and hitting

151

hard under your enemy's jaw. (Your hands will now be in a "natural" position—left at the top end of club, right near bottom end, both thumbs up.) Retain the two-handed grip. See Figure 60a.

3. Bring your left hand up so that the club is in a horizontal position and strike down with the middle part of the club hard on the bridge of your enemy's nose.

4. Strike forward with the club (still horizontal—two-handed grip) hitting your enemy's throat a very hard blow with the middle portion of the club. Figure 60b.

This fighting sequence makes it fairly hard for the enemy to grab the club especially if worked fast and if you land the first blow. Landing any one of these blows hard would probably stun an enemy enough to immobilize him temporarily and let you finish him.

R.D. 4443

Figure 60(a).—Club—Fighting Sequence—Part 1.

Figure 60(b).—Club—Fighting Sequence—Part 2.

d. **Club Strangle.**—This is a very quick and noiseless strangle which can be used from the rear on an unsuspecting person such as a sentry.

1. Using the "short hold" on the club (assume it is held in right hand) approach enemy from behind with wrists crossed and "long" end of club forward and to the right.

2. Slip the "long" end of the club across his windpipe from the left and grab the end with your left hand.

3. Draw your hands and arms toward you strongly. You will pull the club against his windpipe and

your crossed forearms will force his neck against the club in a shearing action. Help bring him down by a hard, quick knee in the back or foot on the back of his knee. See Figure 61.

Turn to and practice club work for about 6-8 minutes.

Assemble for demonstration of come-alongs with the club.

R.D. 4443

Figure 61.—Club Strangle.

e. **Club Come-Alongs.**—Instructor's Note: These are of general interest to the course and probably of no value as far as the enemy is concerned. They are taught only when time permits. They may be useful for breaking up fights, quieting drunks, and the like. (This should be explained to the candidates.)

(1) **Under Arm Method.**—1. Approach opponent from left rear with the club held horizontally under your right armpit with about 1½ feet protruding forward. Have your left hand advanced near the club and your right hand down and slightly forward. Figure 62a.

2. Draw his left hand out with your left hand and slip the club inside of his left arm. Bring his left forearm back towards his body and forward and up so that he encloses the club within his left elbow. At the same time bring your right hand up from below and grasp the club near the front end, trapping his left wrist. Maintain your grip on the club with your right armpit. See Figure 62b.

3. Bear up and to the left, hard with your right wrist thus forcing the bony part of his wrist and forearm into the club. At the same time you can raise up on the entire club by using your body. See Figure 62c. This will encourage your opponent beyond all description to "come-along". The only persons upon whom this come-along is ineffective are those with very muscular forearms and wrists.

Figure 62(a).—Club Come-Along—Under Arm—Part 1.

Figure 62(b).—Club Come-Along—Under Arm—Part 2.

Figure 62(c).—Club Come-Along—Under Arm—Part 3.

(2) **Side of Arm Come-Along.**—1. Same as in Under Arm Method.

2. Place the club along opponent's left elbow from the outside catch his left hand in yours, and reach inside of his left arm with your right arm. See Figure 63a.

3. Catch the front end of the club with your right hand (palm down), and at the same time bring his left hand up and back past his shoulder, bearing down on the club with your right hand and armpit as you do. See Figure 63b. Your opponent will experience convincing pain in his elbow and shoulder.

Figure 63(a).—Club Come-Along—Side of Arm—Part 1.

Figure 63(b).—Club Come-Along—Side of Arm—Part 2.

(3) **Crotch Come-Along.**—1. Grasp the club in the center with your right hand.

2. Slip the club between your opponent's legs from the rear and lift up hard so that the club between your opponent's legs is horizontal and is binding the front of his thighs. At the same time grab the scruff of his collar on his left arm.

3. Walk your opponent away by keeping the club raised high. He will be off balance and unable to run or maneuver. See Figure 64.

Practice come-alongs for rest of hour.

R.D. 4443

Figure 64.—Club Come-Along—Crotch.

SECTION 5

COMPETITIVE GAMES AND EXERCISES

23. Eighth Hour of Combat Conditioning Program.—
Notes for Instructors.—Company in sawdust square and vicinity.

1st Platoon—Abdominal Rises—10 minutes.

2d Platoon—Obstacle Course—10 minutes.

3d Platoon—Sawdust Pit—Dives, Rolls, and Falls— 10 minutes.

a. Rotate by platoons every 10 minutes. Total time 30 minutes. Then the company will assemble in the sawdust square in platoons areas for work with pushups, knee bends, rooster fight, and horseback fight controlled by platoon instructors. Time: 10—15 minutes.

(1) **Pushups.**—Done by entire platoon in unison from prone position on commands "Up" and "Down." Do ten pushups, rest a minute, and then fifteen more.

(2) **Knee bends.**—Do twenty of, Section 2, Paragraph 10 l, Physical Training Definitions. (Page 35.)

(3) **Rooster Fight.**—Each man in platoon hold left ankle with left hand, hopping around on right foot; try and knock each other down with shoulders.

(4) **Horseback Fight.**—Men paired off, one "horse" and one rider. Position of rider is on "horse's" shoulders. At given signal all teams try to knock or pull each other down.

b. If time remains, run a relay foot-race between platoons, each man running about 40-50 yards and back. The high and low track hurdles can be used if desired.

c. There are many other useful games other than those described above and those described on the next pages. Those we have included are some of the best that are known in this country. Officers and noncommissioned officers that are interested can usually find or invent more if the need arises.

24. Supplementary Games and Exercises.—To be used whenever time permits or to be substituted for other scheduled exercises and games if desired.

a. **Log Drill.**—(1) Log drill is a vigorous and interesting system of exercise, in which a squad of men manipulates a middle-sized log in unison. The drill is both recreational and body-building. The competition between squads as teams, each with a log, will help bring out the best results from the drill. The logs can be any medium-weight wood about an average of one foot in diameter and about twenty-five feet in length. The actual number of men to a log will be governed by the weight of the log. Each man should handle a load of about sixty to one hundred pounds. The men on each log should all be of about the same height, otherwise the tall men will get more than their share of the load.

(2) **Log Lifting Exercise.**—Conducted by the numbers.

Position of the Squad: In a single file at attention adjacent to right side of the log.

"ONE"   Face left, dropping to the right knee, and grasp the log—left hand under, right hand over.

"TWO"   Stand up, facing right (to the original front) and raising the log to the left hip.

"THREE"   Raise the log and set it on the left shoulder.

"FOUR"   Raise the log overhead, arms straight.

"FIVE"   Lower the log to the right shoulder.

"SIX"   Lower the log to the right hip.

"SEVEN"   Drop left knee to the deck, facing right as you do, and lower the log to the right knee.

"EIGHT"   Lower the log to the deck.

(3) The drill should be executed with plenty of pep but should not be rushed. It may be conducted by instructors or by Candidates for the squad or the platoon. When the men know the positions assumed for each number then the drill can be mixed up at will provided that the moves follow in sequence or in reverse sequence. For example, the commands might run something like this: "One, two, one, two, three, four, three, two, three, four, five, four, five, six, five, four, five, six, seven, six, seven, eight."

(4) **Log-Tossing.**

Formation: Squad in two equal ranks facing each other at about 6-9 feet distance depending upon the weight of the log and number of men. One rank will hold the log chest high. They will count in unison "One, Two, Three," and throw it high in the air towards the opposite rank on "THREE." The opposite rank will catch it and then toss it back in the same manner. Each rank will try to throw it higher than the other. The log-tossing exercise can also be executed by single squads tossing the log out and letting it land on the deck.

(5) **Log Press.**

Position: One squad, minus two men, lying on their backs, bodies perpendicular to and head touching the log, arms at sides. One man standing at each end of the log. The "end" men will then lift the log up and place it across the chests of the rest of the squad who will support it with their hands, palms up. The end men then get down into position with the rest of the squad.

"UP"	The squad presses the log straight up by straightening their arms.
"BACK"	They bring the log back down in an arc and to the deck, arms well extended over their heads. Keep arms extended all the way.
"UP"	Bring the log back in an arc to the "UP" position.
"DOWN"	Lower the log to the original chest position.

(6) **Knee Bends with Log.**

Position: Log on men's shoulders. Deep knee bends in unison, keeping backs straight.

(7) **Log Tunnel—Race.**—Run between squads over a prearranged distance.

Position: Squad in column holding the log about ½′ off the deck and straddling it. Line the front ends of the log up at the starting line. On the signal "GO," the men pass the log backwards through their legs as fast as possible. As soon as the front end of the log clears the "front" man, he runs around to the rear of the squad and straddles the rear end of the log. The log passing and leap-frogging continues and the race is finished when the front end of the log crosses the finish line.

(8) **Log Foot Race.**—The race can be run between squads over a given distance or it can be run with squad relays between platoons. Each squad will have a log. Passing of logs between relays is not necessary. The men must be careful that no one is in the way when they drop the logs to the deck. The men will be instructed that they can hold and run with the log in any manner that they want to provided no part of the log in any manner touches the ground. That will be all that is told them except to designate the course. Let their initiative do the rest. There are actually many possible ways to carry the log, such as with men on either side, holding the log against hips or resting on locked arms. They can also hold the log overhead or on their shoulders. A good way to hold the log is for all hands to face it and hold it on their arms, chest high, running with the log moving laterally instead of lengthwise.

(9) For both races and for all competitive work involving a number of teams or individual competitors, the watchword should be **"Don't be last."** The instructor might explain that not everybody could be first but that to be last was a disgrace and a justification for good-natured ridicule as well as a forfeit (performance of some exercise or stunt) for the amusement of everybody that wasn't last.

b. **Mass Exercises Given from Formations for Physical Drill to a Squad, Platoon, or Company.**—(1) **Knee Bends.**—This exercise is excellent for toning and developing the thigh muscles.

Position: Hands and arms straight to the front. Feet together.

1. Flex one-third of the way.
2. Flex knees another third of the way.
3. Flex knees completely (full squat).
4. Come up to standing position.

Do 10—20 of these. Start with 10 the first time and work up.

(2) **Squat-Jumps.**—A favorite of the U.S. Navy and a splendid all-around exercise for the legs. A surprisingly good leg workout can be obtained in one minute's time with this exercise.

Position: Hands clasped behind the head; left foot about twelve inches ahead of the right; body in a full squat, sitting on haunches; back fairly straight.

Exercise: 1. Spring straight up in the air, straightening out the legs and having the feet come off the deck a couple inches. While in the air, change the position of the feet. Land on the feet, right twelve inches ahead of left, knees bent, and go right down to the full squat position.

2. Repeat (1) by springing up, changing feet position and settling back to full squat. Keep back fairly erect and hands clasped behind head.

Continue the exercise making the movements continuous and "bouncing" up automatically upon landing. Allow one (1) count for each jump. All hands will count out loud, consecutively, as they execute the exercise fairly slowly. Start with about fifteen (15) Squat-jumps and work up to thirty (30).

(3) **Push-Ups.**

Position: Body supported from deck by hands and toes, face down. Back, arms, and legs straight.

1. Lower body one-third of the way to the deck. Keep back and legs straight.
2. Lower body another third of the way to the deck.
3. Lower body until chest touches the deck.
4. Come up to starting position.

Do 10—20 of these. Start with 10 the first few times and work up.

A fine exercise for the arms and shoulders. Also it helps the back and stomach muscles.

(4) **Press-Press-Fling.**

Position: Arms completely flexed and horizontal; elbows out to sides and slightly forward; fingers extended and joined, palms down touching upper chest; shoulders normal, head erect.

"PRESS"	Keeping arms flexed, swing the elbows way back in vigorous horizontal arcs, moving the shoulders to the rear. Return automatically to position.
"PRESS"	Same as before.
"FLING"	Fling the arms way out and to the rear in vigorous horizontal arcs. This is the same as a "press" except that the arms are not kept flexed but are straightened vigorously. Return to position automatically.

Execute with a lot of snap and vigor. Be sure and keep the head erect, chin in, and back straight while performing the exercise. The exercise can be given 10-20 times, starting with 10 the first time and working up. This is a good exercise for the chest and shoulders. It also is fine for the arms.

(5) **Up, Back, and Over.**

Position: Position of Attention except that palms of hands are to the rear. Keep arms and hands extended at all times.

"UP"	Raise the extended arms up and overhead in vertical arcs to the front.
"BACK"	Swing arms from the shoulders forward, down and way back in vertical arcs.
"OVER"	Swing the arms forward and up as before but this time spread the arms a little when going overhead and swing the arms all the way over and down behind, coming automatically forward to the "UP" position.

The instructor will give the commands "UP," "BACK," "OVER" several times and then give **"ALL THE WAY."** When this command is given then just knock off the "Back" phase and rotate the extended arms continuously "UP and OVER."

The instructor may then give, at any time, **"REVERSE,"** upon which command your arms will rotate in the same way as before—but in reverse direction. He may also give, at any time, **"TIGHTEN 'EM UP."** This means to rotate the extended arms about a horizontal axis to the sides in smaller and faster arcs than before. **"FASTER"** may come next and means simply to speed up the rotation of your arms. The exercise is halted after 1—2 minutes.

(6) **Circle Drill.**—A game that is excellent for a platoon or even a company to participate in is Circle Drill.

Formation: All hands form a large circle with about five or six foot intervals between them. They are then started double-timing around in a circle, waiting for the instructor's commands and reacting as follows:

"HIT THE DECK"	Simply hit the deck fast.
"UP"	Get up fast and start double-timing in the original direction.
"REVERSE"	Turn and run in reverse direction.
"PIGGY-BACK"	Everybody tries to scramble onto someone else's back as fast as possible. All those who are not paired up after the instructor blows his whistle must go into the center of the circle to pay a forfeit.
"GROUPS OF THREE"	(Or any other number up to nine.) Everyone tries to form a tight circle of three men as fast as possible. Any persons left over after the whistle has blown must pay a forfeit as before.
"SQUADS"	This is a good one to spring after the men are all mixed up. The men must all get into a quick squad huddle. After the whistle blows any stowaways in foreign squads and any persons not already in their own squad huddle must come into the center of the circle, and also the entire squads that these men belong to, to pay a forfeit.

(7) For the paying of forfeits, the instructor will first suggest a few such as "Ten Deep Knee-Bends" or "Ten Push-ups" and will then call for suggestions from the men and render sentence in accordance with the popular acclaim. If there are enough men to pay the forfeit, then a more difficult one can be assigned such as sprinting 100—200 yards or duck-waddling 50—75 yards "quacking" all the way. As before the watchword should always be, "Don't be last!"

SECTION 6

KNIFE

25. Ninth Hour of Combat Conditioning Program.—Company assembled in area between bayonet and obstacle courses. Equipment will be M1 Bayonets, scabbards fixed.

    a. **Use of Knife, General.**—Section Instructor: The knife is a standard piece of equipment in line units of the Marine Corps both for utility purposes such as hacking brush and opening C-Ration cans, and as a last-resort fighting weapon. The knife has actually been used by Marines in hand-to-hand fighting in this war—perhaps not on a large scale but nevertheless in many instances where other weapons were gone or on night infiltration missions requiring stealth. It must of course be borne in mind that the enemy is equipped with knives for fighting and knows how to use them, and therefore all Marines in the field should be able to defend themselves against knife attack as well as to use the knife offensively.

    b. **Types of Knives.**—The types of knives you may run into in the field are these three (display them): The short bayonet, which can be used as a knife; the regulation service knife; and the stilletto. See Figure 65.

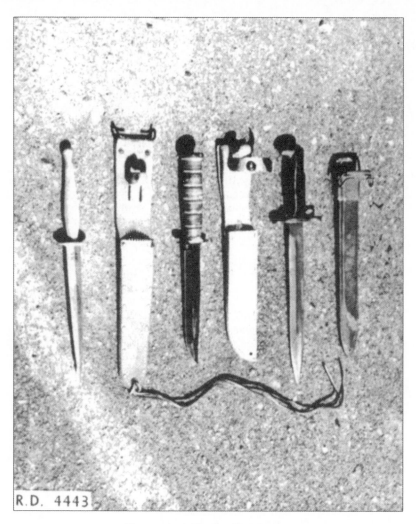

R.D. 4443

Figure 65.—Knife—Types of.

(1) **The Short Bayonet** (M1 Bayonet).—This will in all probability be used by rifle troops for utility as well as for bayonet and knife fighting and should supplant all other bayonets in the Marine Corps infantry units. It will be supplemented by the service knife which is still being issued to the infantry. You are all familiar with the M1 Bayonet and its ruggedness and cutting ability. You will appreciate it even more when you get into our bayonet training. It is, of course, single-edged with part of the square edge sharpened in addition.

(2) **The G. I. Service Knife.**—A sturdy knife which has been issued in the past few months to all line units. It is excellent as an all-purpose knife and can cut vines, open

cans, shave off beards, and kill Japs if properly used and cared for. It comes in an issue leather sheath. Even though we now have the short bayonet, the G. I. Knife is still issued regularly to infantry troops. Aviators, artillerymen, and the like carry them too. It is still valuable as a last-resort weapon. This knife is single-edged, like the short bayonet and is heavy enough to slash with by a flick of the wrist. The handle is round and fairly large.

(3) **The Stiletto.**—A specialized fighting knife that was issued to the Raider Battalions for use in their specialized lethal work. It is a light-weight, double-edged knife with a slender, round, tapering grip which makes for ease in grasping and manipulating the knife. Also it has a short guard which projects all the way around the handle which the G. I. Knife does not have. It is completely double-edged and made of high-tempered and fairly brittle steel. It is too light in weight to slash with by flicking the wrist, but is well adapted for other types of slashing and for thrusting, which many utility knives are not. The knife is too light and brittle for utility work but is excellent for fighting provided there are no heavy clothes to penetrate. It is of no particular interest to the Marine infantry.

(4) A Marine normally carries a knife in a place of ready access on his belt or in his clothing where it won't be seen by an attacking enemy but where he can get it unlimbered in a hurry.

c. **Grip.**—(1) To grasp a knife for fighting purposes lay the grip of the knife diagonally across the palm in this manner (Demonstrate) and close your fingers around it firmly but not too tensely. Notice that your second, third, and fourth fingers will each be wrapped around the grip more than the index finger. The thumb should press straight along the handle and should point up towards the blade. Thumb and index finger will be just inside the guard. If the blade is single edged, the blade can face either inboard or outboard as you will see presently. Figure 66.

(2) The diagonal grip will give you maximum control and effectiveness with the knife. Avoid an overhand grip like this (demonstrate) or an underhand grip like this (demonstrate). They are too limited in their usefulness to be considered. Some people fight with grips like these. However, they are good for only one or two particular strokes, whereas the "diagonal" grip is flexible and good for almost anything.

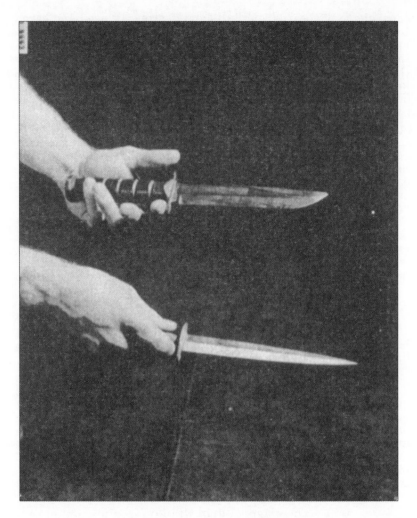

Figure 66.—**Grip on Knife.**

d. **Stance.**—The recommended stance for knife fighting is that similar to a boxer's (with one foot advanced) or to a wrestler's (with the feet more or less in line), whichever is best for the individual. In any event the feet are comfortably apart, weight distributed evenly on the ball of both feet, knees flexed and body bent somewhat forward from the waist, poised and ready to react swiftly in any direction. Needless to say, your eyes are always on your enemy. The knife is held about waist high and close to the body, the blade pointing at your enemy's torso. The other hand is extended in front of the body as bait, also to ward off any advances that the enemy might make, or to grab him somewhere and work into an opening for a quick thrust or slash. Figure 67.

Figure 67.—Stance for Knife Fighting.

e. **Where to Strike.**—(1) (Instructor breaks out a dummy stuffed with straw and demonstrates). The parts of the body most vulnerable to **thrusts** are the abdomen, the throat (especially near the base) and the kidneys. The thorax is of course a vital spot because of the heart and lungs within. However, it is not quite as vulnerable to a thrust as are the aforementioned spots because of the possibility of the knife

173

getting tangled up in a rib before getting into "pay dirt." For any of the spots mentioned, a penetration of three inches is plenty to do a fatal job.

(2) **Slashes.**—For slashes the first place to think of is the throat. Here it must be remembered that cutting the windpipe is often not enough, but that the jugular vein(s) or the thyroid gland(s) must be severed as well. A good slash in this region is, of course, fatal. Other exposed areas where slashing is very effective though perhaps not fatal are: the hands, especially if he has a knife or club; the thighs near the knee joint where a good slash will hamstring your enemy; the armpits and chest and back muscles in the immediate vicinity, where a good cut may immobilize an arm; the face, especially the eyes and forehead where running blood from a slash will help blind your enemy; the crotch which is, as you know, a vital area; and to a lesser extent the insides of the wrists which are not too well exposed but where a slash may incapacitate a hand and incidentally will eventually cause death through arterial hemorrhage. These then are the spots that are most easily exposed for slashing. If in the course of the melee you get a chance to slash anywhere—arm, chest, back or anywhere else—you will naturally strike instinctively. The cuts all add up to weaken your enemy, but chances are you won't be able to wait that long, so get to a vital spot as soon as possible and sink the steel in.

(3) **Knife Strokes** (Demonstrate on straw dummy).—The strokes that you want to become adept at are the thrusts and slashes.

(4) **The Knife Thrust.**—Keep the wrist rigid and let the knife be just an extension of your arm. Execute the thrust to the exposed vital spot by shooting the arm out and driving the knife from its initial position in the vicinity of the waist straight to its mark. Such a thrust might be delivered to the abdomen or throat or to the kidney if his side were exposed. In withdrawing from a thrust, do not simply pull the blade straight out but twist it sharply as you withdraw it so that you enlarge the wound appreciably. You can, as an alternative, slash vigorously as you withdraw from the thrust.

(5) **Knife Slashes.**—Slashes can be made with either the tip end of the blade or with a cutting edge. The best type of slash to use depends upon the knife, its weight and its cutting edges.

(6) In general a single-edged knife is appreciably heavier than a double-edged knife of the same size. The single-edged knife can be used for slashing with either the tip end of the blade or with the single cutting edge. Double-edged knives are generally too light to slash with the tip of the blade but are excellent for pull-slashing with either cutting edge.

174

(7) **The Tip of Blade Slash.**—This is usually executed only with knives which have fairly heavy blades—usually single-edged knives. Recall the fighting grip. You should have the knife grip held diagonally across your palm, **the cutting edge outboard,** and your **palm down.** From this position you can reach out and shoot the blade to its mark (at thigh or the throat) and can slash the spot twice with the tip of your blade by flicking your wrist and swinging your arm horizontally to the right, then turning your hand over (by rotating it clockwise 180°) and flicking your wrist and arm back to the left. Notice that you flick your wrist the same way in respect to your forearm each time and that you only need a single edged blade for this type of slash. The slash is a very fast one and can be very effective. The short bayonet and the G. I. knife are particularly well adapted for this slash. The tip-of-blade slash can be executed with a double-edged knife without turning the wrist over before the slash back.

(8) **The Pull Slash.**—This slash can be made with either a double-edged blade or a single-edged one held with the **palm down, cutting edge inboard.** The knife becomes an extension of the arm. The blade tip or the cutting edge is laid across the exposed part and the knife is pulled across the area forcing the blade in deep. Notice that it is much easier for you to **pull** the blade (flex arm to demonstrate) than to **push** it (extend arm) across the exposed area because of the nature of your grip, your thumb being the weakest part of it. (This is true particularly when the blade is in deep and when the slashing movement is done relatively slowly. A fast, tip-of-blade slash has all the knife's momentum to help as well as the impetus of your wrist and arm.) Whenever you have finished a slashing stroke, turn the blade over in the wound and pull back sharply in the opposite direction slashing him again!

f. **Knife Attack.**—(1) In attacking an enemy with a knife, a lot will depend upon his weapons, if any, and his defense. Naturally you wouldn't openly attack a man armed with a firearm, but you might go up against a man armed with a knife or club. Keep your knife close to your body in instant readiness for a thrust or slash, and make an opening. You can **feint** with your knife, as you come in, that is fake a slash or thrust high and then actually slash or thrust low or vice versa. You can likewise feint to one side. (Demonstrate).

(2) You may be able to catch a hand, arm or elbow (demonstrate) and pull your enemy's side or armpit to you, exposed for a fast thrust or slash. See Figure 68. Also you may be able to rush your enemy, planting your left forearm up against his waist thus preventing him from getting to your knife to block it and then slashing up into the crotch with the knife. Then too a very effective move is start a thrust straight towards his body but veer it sharply to one side and then slash back to the opposite side against his body

or his hand or wrist, should he have moved his hand out to stop your feinted thrust. Whatever you do, do not commit your entire weight in a blow until your enemy is down or there is otherwise no chance of his defending himself. Remember that there will be little time for fencing, so close in quickly, feint or force an opening and get in a good blow to some vulnerable spot, working quickly up to a fatal stroke in a vital spot.

R.D. 4443

Figure 68.—Knife Attack.

g. **Taking Down a Sentry From Behind.**—On infiltration missions it may be necessary to take down a sentry quietly and dispose of him without giving yourself away. A knife can be used for that purpose very effectively. Holding the knife for the "pull" slash (i.e., if it is single-edged; if double-edged, immaterial) crawl up to sentry from behind getting within six feet of him if possible. Come up quietly off the ground and spring to him quickly but silently, clapping your left hand over his mouth, pinching his nostrils between your left thumb and forefinger and pull slashing straight across his windpipe with your knife. Have a knee in his back as you do this and try and get him down before he drops his rifle or anything else he might have in his hands. Figure 69. If taken by surprise the sentry will be unable to emit an outcry (because of hand over mouth and nose and because of severed windpipe), nor should he be able to struggle.

Turn to and practice all of the foregoing (stance, grips, vital spots, strokes, feints, openings and takedown of sentry) in platoon areas. (10 minutes).

Figure 69.—Taking Down a Sentry.

h. **Defense Against Knife Attack.**—(1) The only times you need be concerned with defending yourself against an attacker armed with a knife is when you have no firearms or when your enemy catches you so suddenly that you have no chance to use them. These two situations are quite possible in close-quarter fighting and at night so it is well that you should prepare yourself to be able to meet them. You may have a knife or a club to meet the knife-fighter with. If you do, you are more or less on equal terms. Our main interest at present is how an unarmed man can defend himself against a knife attack.

178

(2) There are several ways to defend yourself against a knife attack if you are bare-handed. If the knife-fighter appears to know his business and to be intent on carrying it out with a vengeance, your best bet is to turn tail and run—get away from him. Then get some weapon or other assistance. Of course, this won't always be possible. The next best thing to do is to pick up a handful of dirt and throw it into his eyes as he closes in, rushing him, grabbing for the knife hand, and kicking and kneeing him in any exposed vital spots. Figure 70. You can grab anything available to throw in his face—rocks, sticks, even your cap or helmet. If you can whip off your jacket fast enough you can use it as a shield to tangle the knife up in.

You can try and kick him hard in the crotch or knees with your foot and leg well extended like this. (Demonstrate kicking technique from a distance: balance on outboard foot, keep body bent away from opponent, lash way out with inboard foot.) If you can't do any of these things, then you have the unpleasant job of trying to disarm him barehanded.

Figure 70.—Defense Against Knife Attack.

i. **Knife Disarming.**—(1) **General.**—This is generally a last resort in defense against knife attack. If you are caught unawares it may have to be the first thing you attempt. Knife disarming is quite difficult and dangerous to work on a man who is adept with his blade. Even with a man who is holding and using his knife poorly you may get cut a bit before you can disarm him. However, it is much better to come out of the scrap with cut forearms or shoulders than a cut throat or belly. The disarming moves we are about to teach you will minimize the danger of getting badly hurt and will at least give you a fighting chance of coming out of the fight the winner and in one piece. The moves require conscientious practice to attain speed and accuracy even though they are quite simple and effective.

(2) **Defense Against Overhand Stab.**—An overhand stab is an ineffective blow unless the victim is caught completely off guard. It looks good in the movies and the opera but as far as we are concerned it is quite easily parried and from it a take-away easily executed. It can be parried with the cross wrist parry or with a forearm parry. The former is usually safer and more effective; the latter is good if attacked from the rear. Both will be considered.

(3) **The Cross Wrist Parry.**—Extend the arms tensely up and in front of the body with the right wrist crossed tightly over the left and with the fingers together and extended, palms to the front. The head should be back, eyes on the knife, the body crouched, knees well bent, right knee in front of crotch. Catch the enemy's descending "knife wrist" between your crossed wrists and as high up as possible. (See Figure 71.) This will stop a hard overhand stab before it can do much damage, and breaks from it come naturally no matter which hand the knife is held in. With a little reflection it should be evident that the higher up you can stop your enemy's knife hand, the easier it will be to get him under control.

Figure 71.—Against Overhand Stab, Cross-Wrist Knife Parry.

(4) Using the Cross Wrist Parry the following breaks are recommended: (Assume knife held in enemy's right hand. If it is left just reverse **left** and **right**).

(5) **Grab Knife Wrist, Hit Crotch.**—This is the primary move—simplest and very effective.

1. Block the stab with the cross wrist parry.

2. Grab the enemy's knife wrist with both of your hands and at the same time close in and knee or kick him hard in the crotch.

3. Follow through with foot or knee blows to the crotch, knees, shins, feet, and stomach until he goes down and drops the knife. Finish him off barehanded or with the knife.

181

(6) **Grab with Right Hand—Wristlock.**—This is probably the next best effective move.

     1.   Same as in (5).

     2.   Grab enemy's knife wrist with your right hand. (Note how easily this is done from the crossed wrist position) and at the same time bring your left arm up behind his right upper arm, bring your left hand forward and grab your right wrist. See Figure 72a.

     3.   Pull down with your left hand and wrist bending back his knife arm in a lever-like action and keeping the knife close to his head. Slam your right forearm and elbow into your adversary's throat, and at the same time bring up your right knee into his crotch hard. See Figure 72b.

R.D. 4443

Figure 72(a).—Grab with Right Hand—Wrist Lock—Part 1.

Figure 72(b).—Grab with Right Hand—Wrist Lock—Part 2.

(7)   Alternate to (6)—**Grab Wrist, Elbow Break.**
    1.   Same as in (5).
    2.   Grab his knife wrist with your right hand and pull it across to your right, keeping the blade away from you as much as possible. At the same time come up and to the right hard with the palm of your left hand underneath his right elbow straightening it out. Figure 73a.
    3.   Work him down fast by twisting his wrist with your right hand clockwise and pushing down hard with your left and on the back of his right elbow. Stay fairly well

away from him and keep the knife clear of you. A knee pressed on his right shoulder will help him go down. Figure 73b.

  4. Land hard on his kidney (whichever one is exposed) with your left knee. As an alternative you can land on his knife arm just short of the shoulder and break it. Finish him off with the knife should he drop it or with your left hand and knee otherwise.

Figure 73(a).—Grab with Right Hand—Elbow Break—Part 1.

Figure 73(b).—Grab with Right Hand—Elbow Break—Part 2.

(8) **Grab Wrist with Left Hand—Arm Lock.**
1. Same as in (5).
2. Grab his knife wrist with your **left** hand and at the same time reach underneath his right upper arm with your right arm bring your right hand up and lay it upon the back of your left hand.
3. Bear back against his right wrist with both your hands using your right arm as a lever and keeping the knife away from your face. At the same time knee him in the crotch with your right knee or rear leg trip him and land on his right side with your right knee. Figure 74.

Turn to and practice simulating knife defense by throwing sand, rocks, cap or helmet, by using a club and by use of the foot in kicking. Then practice the four disarming moves just explained and demonstrated. (10-15 minutes).

Assemble the company. Answer any questions on material or moves thus far.

Figure 74.—Grab with Left Hand—Arm Lock.

(9) **Forearm Parries.**—A left or right-handed overhand stab can also be parried with a single forearm. This is particularly useful when the attacker comes at you from the rear and you just barely have time to whirl about, duck down, and step in, coming up with the nearest forearm raised and horizontal and blocking his knife from hitting you just as effectively as will the cross-wrist parry. But it is somewhat harder to perform a take-away from this parry than from the cross-wrist parry.

Breaks Using the Forearm Parry—(Assume knife in right hand. For left hand simply reverse **right** and **left**).

186

(10) Right Forearm Parry—Wrist Lock.

1. Block the descending knife wrist with your upraised right forearm ducking your head. Keep your knees bent, right knee protecting your crotch, and your body crouched.

2. Bring your left arm up behind his right upper arm and grab your right wrist with your left hand, forcing his knife wrist back past his shoulder.

NOTE: If the enemy is fast (after the knife stab is blocked) and tries to disengage his wrist by drawing the knife back up, he is simply making it that much easier for you to get the wrist lock; if he is smart and tries to straighten out his arm, slip the knife around your arm, and come down to your side with a stab, all you have to do is catch hold of his knife wrist with your right hand and continue with the wrist lock. Even if he succeeds in getting his arm partially straightened out, you can still pass your left arm up behind his right forearm and catch your right wrist with your left hand, thus securing the knife hand, and then follow through as in 4.

3. Using your left forearm as a lever, bear his knife hand (keeping the knife away from you) back past his right shoulder and at the same time drive your right forearm and elbow into his throat. This will start him down.

4. Knee him in the crotch and when he lands, land on his side with your right knee. Continue pressure on his arm and finish him with your knees or with the knife when he drops it.

(11) Left Forearm Parry—Wrist Lock.

1. Same as in (10) except use **left** forearm.

2. Bring your right arm up behind his right upper arm, grab your left wrist or hand and bear back with a lever-like action on his knife wrist forcing it past his right shoulder. Be sure and press your left elbow in to meet your right elbow thus keeping his knife arm secure!

NOTE: If you do not do this quickly enough he can straighten out his knife arm and stab you in the kidney before you can do anything. For this reason it is preferable to **block a right-hand stab with your right forearm and a left with a left.**)

3. Same as move No. 4 in (10).

Turn to and practice these last two disarming moves for the rest of the hour.

26. 10th Hour of Combat Conditioning.—Line the company up at the south edge of the sawdust pit and roll back and forth a few times across the pit. (4-5 minutes). Then leave the pit, move over to area south of pit and break up into platoons for a scheduled workout as follows:

1st Platoon—Abdominal Rises—6 minutes.

2d Platoon—Obstacle Course—6 minutes.

3d Platoon—Crab Drill and Pushups—6 minutes.

Platoon instructors stay with platoons. Rotate twice and finish up. Total time, 18-20 minutes.

Company assembles again in area between obstacle and bayonet courses and finishes up on Knife Disarming.

a. **Knife Disarming.**—Section Instructor: First of all, are there any questions on the knife work we have considered and practiced so far?—All right, we will now take up disarming moves for thrusts.

(1) **Disarming for a Straight Knife Thrust.**—This is somewhat difficult to execute, especially if a thrust is made very rapidly or if your opponent has hold of you with one hand, preventing you from dodging the knife. If he should have hold of you, then grab quickly for his knife hand with one or both of your own and then get your knees and feet busy on his crotch, knees, shins, and feet. If he does not have hold of you but starts a thrust, execute this move:

(2) **Step to Side—Elbow Break.**—Assume knife in enemy's right hand. If held in left simply reverse "left" and "right."

1. With your right foot step quickly backward and to the left, pivoting on the ball of your left foot and getting your body out of the way of the thrust. At the same time swing your left arm sharply to the right hitting his knife arm with your forearm and deflecting the thrust to the right.

2. Grab his knife hand with your right, laying the palm of your hand against the back of his hand, and twist his hand clockwise bending his hand back (palm towards wrist). See Figure 75a. At the same time come up and to the right hard underneath his right elbow with the heel of your left hand straightening out the elbow.

3. Bear down hard on his elbow with your left hand and continue to twist and raise his knife hand, thus forcing him down to the deck. Assist with the left knee on his arm just short of the shoulder if necessary. Keep the knife clear of you. See Figure 75b.

4. Land hard on his side with your knee or on his right upper arm dislocating his shoulder or breaking the arm. Follow through.

R.D. 4443

Figure 75(a).—**Against Straight Thrust, Step to Side—Elbow Break—**
Part 1.

R.D. 4443

Figure 75(b).—Against Straight Thrust, Step to Side—Elbow Break—
Part 2.

As an alternate to this move use the following move:
  (3) **Side-to-Side—Hammer Lock.**
    1. Same as in (2).
    2. Grab his knife hand with your right, lay-
ing the palm of your hand against the back of his hand and
twist his hand clockwise, bending his hand back (palm towards
wrist). At the same time come up hard underneath his right
elbow with the heel of your left hand and grab his sleeve.
    3. By twisting and pulling to the left on his
knife hand with your right and pushing up and to the right
on his right elbow with your left hand, work his arm into a

190

hammer-lock, forcing his knife hand up between his shoulder blades. Place your left hand, palm down, upon his right shoulder. Grab his knife hand with your right hand enclosing the knife within his fingers and work the blade into the back of his neck.

NOTE: The first disarming move of these two is probably preferable because it is somewhat less complicated.

(4) **Disarming for a Side Thrust.**—A thrust from the side can also be parried with the forearm either inward or outward.

(5) **Parry Out—Knee Crotch.**—(Assume knife in right hand as before).

1. Parry the knife wrist and forearm outward by coming down and to the left with a sharp sweeping movement of your left arm making contact with your forearm. Figure 76a.

2. Immediately close in rapidly and knee your enemy in the crotch and hit him in the throat with your right fist. Then with your left hand grab his knife wrist and continue to slug, knee, and kick him if he has any fight left. Figure 76b.

Figure 76(a).—Against Straight Thrust, Parry Out Knee Crotch—Part 1.

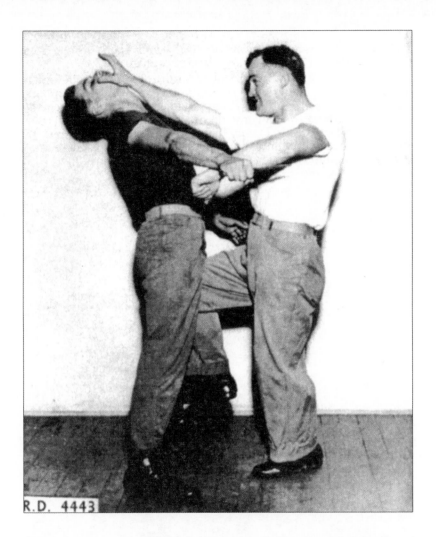

Figure 76(b).—Against Straight Thrust, Parry Out Knee Crotch—Part 2.

(6) **Parry In.**—For this parry you can execute the same two disarming moves that you did for the **straight thrust,** that is, either the **elbow-break** or the **hammer lock.**

(7) Turn to in platoon areas and practice the disarming movement for a straight thrust and for a side thrust. (6-8 minutes).

(8) **Disarming from an Underhand Stab.**—Should your enemy swing an uppercut knife stroke at you aimed for your crotch or belly, react in either of these two ways:

(9) **Cross Wrist Parry—Hammer Lock.**

1. Extend your arms forward and down, wrists crossed (right over left) and catch his up-swinging

193

knife wrist between your wrists. Pull your body to the rear out of the way of the blade as you do. Figure 77a.

       2.   Without hesitation grasp his sleeve underneath his right elbow from the outside with your right hand, and pull it toward you and then to the right. Simultaneously bear forward and to the right on his right hand and wrist with your left wrist so that you bend his arm at the elbow. If this is executed quickly and vigorously it will bend even a strong arm that is resisting the movement. Figure 77b.

R.D. 4443

Figure 77(a).—Against Under Hand Stab, Cross-Wrist Parry—Hammer-lock—Part 1.

Figure 77(b).—Against Under Hand Stab, Cross-Wrist Parry—Hammer-
lock—Part 2.

Figure 77(c). —Against Under Hand Stab, Cross-Wrist Parry—Hammer-
lock—Part 3.

3. Quickly slip your left hand inside of his
right elbow and lay it on the inside of his right upper arm.
Figure 77c. Continue to pull to the right on his elbow with
your right hand. Bear down with your left shoulder and left
hand, helping to bend his arm some more and starting to
force his knife hand up his back between his shoulder blades.
Be careful of the knife.

4. Grab his knife hand with your right hand
enclosing the knife within his fingers and pull it up between
his shoulder blades. Assist this by placing your left hand on
his right shoulder and then bearing down and forward with
your left shoulder, hand, and upper arm.

5. With your right hand force the knife (still trapped in his own right hand) into the back of his neck.

(10) **Double Hand Catch—Arm Drag—Knee Crotch.**

1. Reach down with both arms extended, body pulled back to the rear and catch his up-swinging knife wrist in both hands.

2. Retain your grip on his wrist with the left hand. Release your right hand, reach with it inside of his right armpit and catch hold of his right upper arm near the shoulder. Figure 78a.

3. Push his right wrist vigorously away from you with your left hand, (keeping his right arm straight) pull his right upper arm sharply to you with your right hand, and step in, driving your right knee hard into his crotch. Figure 78b.

4. If this does not finish him, retain your grasp and lever with both hands and keep your feet and knees busy until you do finish him.

(11) Turn to and practice these and the previous disarming movements in platoon areas for about 5-10 minutes. Assemble again and answer any questions.

(12) Instructor's Note: If there is time enough left, run a **Fireman's Carry Race** between platoons.

Figure 78(a).—Against Straight Thrust, Double Hand Catch—
Arm Drag—Knee Crotch—Part 1.

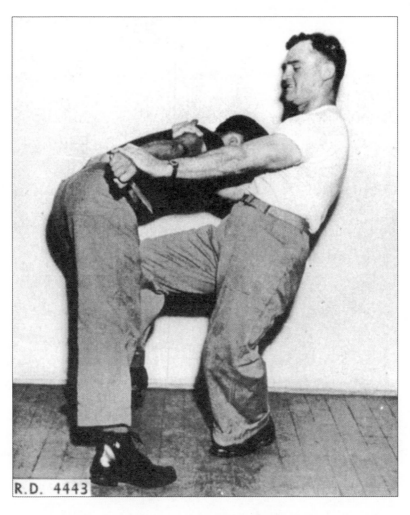

R.D. 4443

Figure 78(b).—Against Straight Thrust, Double Hand Catch—
Arm Drag—Knee Crotch—Part 2.

SECTION 7

BAYONET

27. 11th Hour of Combat Conditioning Program.—a. **Introduction to Bayonet Program.**—(1) Combat Conditioning Instructor: Men, this is going to be your first hour of nine in bayonet training in Candidates' Class. You have all had some training with the bayonet already. When you finish the course here we intend that you shall not only be much more adept at the bayonet, but that you shall also have a lot more respect for the weapon. In addition you will know how to train Marines in its use.

(2) Our course will cover position, stance, footwork, thrusts, buttstrokes, parries, slashes, feints and simple team tactics. The system we teach is a simple unified system that we recommend for the Marine Corps. It embodies what we consider are the best teachings of the Army system and the "Biddle" system of bayonet fighting. During the course you will not only learn the movements progressively but will also try them against each other paired off and finally when unequally matched. We will also have some time devoted to rifle and bayonet disarming. Remember that we want you to give us your wholehearted efforts and attention while you are out here. We will insist upon that! It won't all be drudgery either and when we finish up if there are any men who think they haven't learned something worthwhile we want to hear from them!

b. **Theory of the Bayonet Fighting.**—(1) The bayonet is used in many tactical situations such as in assault, in combat at quarters that are too close for bullets or grenades, on infiltration missions where secrecy must be preserved, on night operations, and as a last resort when on the defense. The bayonet has been used in the past and **is being used today** —perhaps not on a very large scale, but it still is being used, especially in the Central and Southwest Pacific where quarters are frequently close.

(2) But aside from the variety of tactical uses that we mentioned, men gain confidence when they know they are well-trained bayonet fighters. It is true that only a small proportion of men may ever be called upon to use the bayonet in combat. You may say "Well, I may be carrying ammunition, or in a command post, or firing from 400 yards on the enemy— I won't need to know how to use the bayonet." But the significant fact is that hundreds of thousands of Marines are armed with the bayonet and not one of them can be sure that he will never need to fight with it! And no matter where a man is in the combat area if he lacks ability and confidence in his bayonet it is a weakness tinging all his other abilities.

(3) If you were a platoon leader in the attack you would hardly expect an unhesitant assault by your men when you gave the signal if most of them lacked faith in their hand-to-hand fighting effectiveness and felt more secure the farther they were from the enemy. You wouldn't do it yourself. Confidence and effectiveness with the bayonet is not intended to lead to less appreciation of fire weapons. In fact, during the initial stages of a bayonet assault, hip-level firing is recommended. We say that if a man can advance with confidence armed with a bayonet only, then a loaded rifle will increase his confidence and fighting potentialities proportionately.

    c. **Bayonet Technique.**—(1) All right. Now realize that the bayonet is primarily an offensive weapon and that with it aggressiveness will win. Any hesitation, fencing, or delay of a fraction of a second may mean death. A bayonet fighter must attack in a fast relentless assault until his opponent is destroyed. He takes instant advantage of any opening or makes one by parrying his opponent's weapon and drives the blade or butt into him with killing force.

    (2) In our bayonet training we must first know how the bayonet and rifle can be used to disable and kill an enemy. Penetration of three or four inches almost anywhere in the body proper (thorax, back, or abdomen) is usually fatal. Slashing and severing of the jugular vein will also do the job, while a smash on the skull by the rifle butt or smashing the chest above the heart is a pretty sure bet. A man can be quickly disabled, as far as defending himself is concerned, by slashing his thigh muscles, biceps or hands. Remember that!

    (3) Now the next things in bayonet training are stance, grip, footwork, fundamental movements, and accuracy. Throughout we must emphasize the developing of proper form, quickness with the rifle and bayonet, coordination, balance, strength, and endurance. Relaxation and instinctive movements, vital in all athletics and fighting, must be stressed from the start. **Remember that actual bayonet fighting will never be cut-and-dried!** Anything can happen! The moves we teach you will make you proficient in bayonet use and enable you to react instinctively and take instant advantage of any opening. We consider all these moves, sequences, and training methods purely as a means to an end—to make you and your Marines well-rounded bayonet fighters. You must remember too that the bayonet fight may come as the culmination of a long gruelling advance or a determined defense when men are close to exhaustion. Always bear that in mind and press on with all you've got, although all you may have left may be will power.

    (4) The Instructor will now take up basic positions, grip, footwork, jumping, whirl, "straight" parries, and basic thrusts and buttstrokes. He will demonstrate and explain these, pointing out to the men the most common errors

to be avoided. **He will emphasize that in training, the movements must first be learned "by the numbers," but that as soon as they are learned, all but a simple initial command will be dispensed with so that the bayonet students will learn to react by situation and not by commands.**

(5) **General.**—In assuming any position or executing any movement, the bayonet fighter relaxes the muscles not used directly in the effort. He holds the rifle firmly but without tenseness. Tense muscles induce fatigue and retard speed.

(6) By proper emphasis in training, all movements become instinctive. The bayonet fighter strikes automatically at openings and presses the attack relentlessly. He avoids any fixed sequence of movements. He achieves balance in all his movements and constant readiness to strike instantly in any direction and to keep striking until his opponent has been destroyed. At all times he watches his opponent's bayonet and body. The positions and movements described in this section are designed to accomplish these ends.

(7) The bayonet fighter's positions are GUARD, SHORT GUARD, and HIGH PORT. He executes the following basic movements: WHIRL, LONG THRUST, SHORT THRUST, WITHDRAWAL, PARRY RIGHT AND LEFT, VERTICAL AND HORIZONTAL BUTT STROKES, SMASH, SLASH, and OVERHAND BUTTSTROKE. The beginner learns these movements as separate actions. By training, however, he learns to execute them in varying combinations as swift, continuous actions.

(8) **Guard.**—

TO ASSUME THE POSITION OF GUARD:

1. Face the opponent.

2. Leading with the left foot, take a short step and space the feet laterally as well as in depth, left toe pointing toward the opponent, right toe roughly to the right, bending the knees slightly, incline the body slightly forward, hips level.

3. At the same time throw the rifle forward, point of the bayonet moving straight toward the opponent, and catch the rifle with both hands. This movement must be swift and sure.

4. Grasp the rifle with the left hand, palm against the left side of the rifle at the most convenient point forward of the balance, usually just in front of the lower band, with the left arm slightly bent. With the right hand palm to the left, grasp the small of the stock. To prevent bruising the right forefinger, hold the small of the stock so that the finger is not touching the trigger guard. Hold the rifle firmly but not rigidly with both hands, in a natural position. Point the bayonet at the base of the opponent's throat. The butt will be in the vicinity of the hip or thigh. Most persons find a canted

position of the "plane of the rifle" of about 45° to be best. It allows an easy but firm grip and maximum control of rifle and blade by arms and wrists. Moreover when thrusts are made into the thorax with the blade "at an angle" or actually "flat" there is less likelihood of getting the blade stuck between the ribs than if the blade is "vertical." Right forearm along the comb of stock is optional.

     5. Balance the weight of the body on both legs, ready for instant movement in any direction.

     6. Keep the eyes on the opponent's bayonet and body. See Figure 79.

R.D. 4443

Figure 79.—Bayonet—On Guard.

(9) **Short Guard.**—To assume the position of SHORT GUARD from GUARD, bring the rifle back so that the right hand is at the right hip. This is a convenient carrying position when moving through dense woods, brush, trenches, around buildings, or when the enemy may be encountered suddenly at very close quarters. The rifle can be "Hip-fired" from this position.

(10) **Common Errors.**

1. Feet not separated in a well-balanced stance.

2. Hips not facing straight forward.

3. Body too erect.

4. Rifle not held naturally.

5. Left arm straight, or bent too much.

6. Rifle gripped tensely, restraining freedom of movement.

7. Point of bayonet too high, or not pointing towards opponent's throat.

(11) **High Port.**—From the position of guard, without changing the position of the feet or the grasp of the hands on the rifle, carry the piece diagonally across the body, sling to the front, until the left wrist is level with and in front of the left shoulder. This is a position of readiness.

(12) **Jumping Trenches and Hurdling Obstacles.**—

1. Jump, holding the rifle at high port, throw the piece sharply upward and forward from the High Port on taking off, and bring it back on landing. **This jumping will also be practiced with the position of the piece approximately maintained with the left hand alone, leaving the right hand free to assist in clearing the obstacle.** For jumping and vaulting pictures see Figure 116, p. 322 and Figure 108, p. 314.

2. To jump, holding the rifle in the Guard position, snap it up quickly on taking off, maintaining the grasp of the hands, and start the piece down from the highest point in the jump. The piece will be snapped down to Guard Position as the jumper alights.

(13) **Whirl.**—See Figures 79a, b, c, and d.—This movement is used to meet an attacker from the rear. The movement faces a bayonet fighter to the rear rapidly and in a position of readiness and at the same time **gains distance between him and his adversary.** To execute the Whirl from the position of Guard, bring the piece to High Port, whirl to the left about by pivoting on the ball of the left (leading) foot, and resume the position of Guard. When proficient, a bayonet fighter combines these three motions into one continuous and rapid movement.

Figure 79(a).—Whirl—Part 1.

Figure 79(b).—Whirl—Part 2.

Figure 79(c).—Whirl—Part 3.

Figure 79(d).—Whirl—Part 4.

(14) **Long Thrust.**—1. To execute the Long Thrust from the Guard position advance the rear foot and lunge forward, extending the entire body.

2. Complete the extension of the body as the rear foot strikes the ground. During this movement drive the rifle, gripped firmly by both hands and guided by the left hand, forcefully in a straight line at the opponent's throat or other opening on his body. Quickly extend the left arm to its full length so that the bayonet **darts** toward the target. At the instant of full extension, the butt of the rifle may be held inside of and pressed against the right forearm. Bend leading knee, incline the body well forward, and straighten the rear leg. See Figure 80a. Remember your primary target, **your enemy's throat**—exposed, vulnerable, and unprotected by clothing.

3. Keep the eyes on the point of attack during the entire movement.

4. If the thrust is evaded, move in swiftly with another thrust, or butt stroke. Retraction and recovery after the thrust will be instantaneous. **There must never be any lingering in the extended position.**

5. The power of the Long Thrust comes from the arms, shoulders, back, legs, and weight of the body. The distance from which the Long Thrust is launched depends on the reach and speed of advance of the attacker. The maximum distance for each individual is determined by trial at a partner acting as coach. It is imperative for each Marine to know his reach and be able to judge his attack distance accurately so that his thrust will reach the target. By increasing the number of steps, the Marine will be trained to execute the thrust with either foot forward.

(15) **Common Errors.**

1. "Telegraphing" the thrust by drawing the rifle back just before starting the thrust.

2. Thrust made with the arms alone and not with the power of legs and body.

3. Thrust accompanied by a slight slash, preventing straight forward penetration.

4. Point of bayonet carried too high, or at a lateral angle to target.

5. Body not inclined far enough forward.

6. Loss of balance, caused by taking too long a step.

7. Leading knee not sufficiently bent.

8. Eyes not on the point of attack.

Withdrawal from Long Thrust—

1. To withdraw from the Long Thrust, advance the left foot and jerk the rifle back along the line of penetration with the force and weight of the entire body,

carrying the body to the rear by straightening the forward leg. If necessary, maintain balance by shifting the right foot to the rear. If enemy is down, place one foot on him and withdraw. In any event, withdraw **instantly,** prepared to execute the Short Thrust or a Butt Stroke or assume the position of Guard or Short Guard. Do not linger in the extended position. Figure 80b.

Figure 80(a).—Long Thrust and Withdrawal—Part 1.

Figure 80(b).—Long Thrust and Withdrawal—Part 2.

(16) **Common Errors.**—1. Not making the withdrawal vigorously, caused by using the arms alone to make the withdrawal.

2. Not withdrawing the bayonet back on the line of penetration, caused by allowing the butt of the rifle to drop.

(17) **Short Thrusts and Withdrawals.**—1. Being in the Guard or Short Guard position, or on withdrawal from a Long Thrust, execute the Short Thrust in the same manner as the Long Thrust, except that the **leading** foot is advanced in lunging forward. The Short Thrust is used when an opponent is encountered suddenly or at a range too close for the Long Thrust. **Practice will include executing the Short Thrust with either the right or left foot forward.** See Figure 81a.

2. Withdraw from a Short Thrust in the same manner as from a Long Thrust. Upon completion of the withdrawal, recover to the Guard position, or execute another thrust or butt stroke. See Figure 81b.

Figure 81(a).—Short Thrust and Withdrawal—Part 1.

Figure 81(b).—Short Thrust and Withdrawal—Part 2.

211

(18) **Parries.**—The Straight Parry is an offensive blow used to create an opening by beating the opponent's bayonet out of the way. It is made by a forward and lateral movement of the bayonet with great force and speed. The lateral movement of the blade is limited to the extent necessary to beat the opponent's weapon clear of your body. The momentum of the parry is continued into a thrust or butt stroke. The position of the opponent's weapon will determine the direction that will best create an opening for instant execution of a thrust or butt stroke.

(19) **Straight Parry Right.**—See Figure 82a.

1. Start to lunge forward in a long Thrust.

2. At the same time, thrust the piece diagonally forward and to the right by straightening the left arm in the direction of the parry, moving the butt to the right and keeping the piece parallel to the Guard position. Added force may be obtained by canting the rifle sharply counter-clockwise by a flick of both wrists. Limit the diagonally, forward movement to that necessary to beat the opponent's blade just clear of the body.

3. Continue the Parry into a Long Thrust during the same forward step. As the bayonet strikes the opponent's blade, beating it clear of the body, and at the instant the bayonet glances off of the opponent's weapon, drive it into him in the same continuous movement.

4. To Parry Right preceding a Short Thrust, execute the movement as described above, making the Parry just prior to the forward lunge with the forward foot.

Figure 82(a).—Straight Parries Right and Left—Part 1.

(20) **Straight Parry Left.**—See Figure 82b.—To Parry Left, lunge forward as in the Straight Parry Right, thrust the rifle forward and to the left so that the butt is approximately in front of the left groin, deflecting the opponent's bayonet clear of the body. The Straight Parry Left is followed by a thrust, or by a buttstroke in case the point of the bayonet is not on a line toward the opponent.

(21) **Common Errors.**—1. Failure to use sufficient force and speed, caused by using the arms alone without the weight and momentum of the body.

2. Making a wide sweeping movement, without any forward movement to the piece.

3. Eyes not on the opponent's weapon.

Figure 82(b).—Straight Parries Right and Left—Part 2.

(22) **Buttstrokes and Slashes.—G e n e r a l.—**The bayonet fighter does not use buttstrokes and slashes in combat when it is possible to use a thrust. But he can use them advantageously in many situations, particularly in close-in fighting when there is not enough room to deliver a thrust or immediately after a thrust that has been evaded. When using a buttstroke the fighter can often knee his opponent in the groin, trip him, or kick him in the legs. Buttstrokes and slashes lend themselves especially to fighting in trenches, woods, and brush, or in a general melee when lateral movements are restricted.

(23) **Vertical Buttstrokes Series.—**1. To make the vertical buttstroke from the Guard position step in with the rear foot and, at the same time, drive the butt forward and upward in a vertical arc to the groin, solar plexus, or chin. See Figures 83a, b. Put the force of the whole body into the blow. The vertical buttstroke may also be started from a crouched position so as to hit low points on the opponent's body while offering him a small difficult target. Do not allow the butt to go above chin height at the end of the stroke, as this will expose your body to your enemy.

R.D. 4443

Figure 83(a).—Vertical Buttstroke—Part 1.

Figure 83(b).—Vertical Buttstroke—Part 2.

      2. **Smash.**—See Figure 84.—If the opponent moves backward and the vertical buttstroke misses, step forward swiftly with the right foot and drive the butt at his head, extending the arms fully forward, and bringing up the left foot to retain balance. In practice we smash twice customarily.

      3. **Slash.**—See Figure 85.—If the opponent again retreats out of butt range or falls, continue to advance slashing diagonally downward with the bayonet. Guide the slash toward the junction of the neck and shoulder, hitting either this point or the head, throat, or arms. If the slash misses (note that a miss brings the movement close to the position of Guard), continue the attack vigorously with a thrust or an overhand buttstroke.

Figure 84.—Smash.

Figure 85.—Slash.

4. **Overhand Buttstroke.**—See Figure 86.—
If the opponent is going down, step forward with the right
foot and at the same time strike forward and downward vigorously with the rifle butt, sling to the front, in a vertical or
diagonal arc. This movement can be executed effectively even
if your bayonet is stuck in the ground or if your opponent
has stepped upon it. Come back to Guard position automatically moving the left foot to the front and making sure
that the rifle and blade come **down** to the guard position in
an overhand arc and not a sideward sweeping motion. This
is to prevent easy blocking of the blade and to take advantage
of possible slashing of the enemy with the cutting edge of the
bayonet.

Figure 86.—Overhand Buttstroke.

(24) **Horizontal Buttstroke Series.**—In this series
the plane of the rifle and bayonet is horizontal instead of
vertical.

1. **Horizontal Buttstroke.**—To make the horizontal buttstroke from the Guard position, drive in vigorously, advancing the rear foot, and swing the butt diagonally
upward through an arc to the opponent's head or body. The
swing can be perfectly horizontal if the opening is most exposed to a side, "hook," blow.

2. **S m a s h .**—If the horizontal buttstroke misses because the opponent has moved backward, deliver a smash, maintaining the butt in the same horizontal position. Notice that with butt's long axis horizontal or diagonal there is a better chance of landing a killing blow to the forehead or bridge of nose than if the axis is vertical.

3. **Slash.**—If the smash misses, continue the attack with a slash, executing the movement as directed in the vertical buttstroke series.

4. **Overhand Buttstroke.**—Whether or not the slash landed, follow through with an overhand buttstroke, then come back on Guard.

(25) **Common Errors for Both Buttstroke Series.**

1. Failure to reach out at the opponent.

2. Insufficient force and accuracy.

3. Insufficient Speed.

4. Faulty balance and footwork.

(26) **Note for Instructors:** Platoon instructors then take charge of their respective platoons for Bayonet Drill and take up the basic movements step-by-step. Do this first "by the numbers" and **as soon as all hands know them, "without the numbers" thereafter.** Platoon instruction must be good, instructors participating actively. A lot of spirit and yelling by the men will be encouraged during Bayonet Drill.

d. **Bayonet Drill Formations.**—(Notes for Instructors.)

(1) **General.**—All controlled bayonet practice is conducted from bayonet drill formations of which there are several. The formation selected will depend mainly upon the type of practice being conducted, upon the size of the unit undergoing the practice, the size of the area available for practice, and upon the availability of a loud-speaker.

(2) **Types of Formations.**—The types of bayonet drill formations recommended for various types of drill are:

1. Two Ranks;

2. Four Ranks;

3. Six or More Ranks;

4. Large Circle.

(3) **Two Ranks.**

1. This is the old standby formation for platoon or squad instruction and is often used for initial, basic bayonet drill. It can also be used for contact work in pairs if the unit is fairly small. The platoon or smaller unit is formed in two equal ranks at normal interval. Bayonets are fixed and the instructor designates one man in the rear rank (usually the middle man or an end man) as "base man." This man immediately comes to High Port. The instructor then commands: 1. Form for Bayonet Training, this man (pointing) Base, 2 MOVE. At the command "Move," the base man comes

"On Guard. " The remainder of the men of the rear rank run at High Port to the right and left, respectively, to secure 3-pace intervals, face to the front and come "On Guard" with a loud yell. Each front rank man runs at High Port by the shortest route to a position about ten (10) paces from and immediately in front of his rear rank file, whirls about, and comes "On Guard" with a loud yell.

2. To assemble the group, the instructor commands: 1. Assemble, 2. MARCH. At the command "March," the base man originally designated assumes the position of "attention." All others yell lustily, come to High Port and form on the base man at a run in the original formation, resuming the position of "attention."

3. The Two-Ranks formation is well adapted for types of drill that require frequent "Crossing Over," i.e., exchanging of the original positions of the two ranks. This movement involves the men of each rank infiltrating the other rank as the ranks pass each other at High Port, and to preclude any clashing of bayonets each man will pass the man he "covers" in the opposite rank, with his right side to the other man's right side. Having reached the opposite rank's original position the men of a rank automatically halt, whirl, and come back on guard with a growl.

4. The instructor conducts the drill by voice from a position between the two ranks in the center or near the end of the formation.

(4) **Four Ranks.**

1. This is a formation used for more advanced work in bayonet training, chiefly for "contact" drill with parries and feints. The drill is relatively stationary and requires less space than the two-ranks formation for a unit of the same size. Up to two platoons can be drilled and controlled by voice with this formation.

2. The formation is composed of four equal ranks at about 3-pace interval and 4-pace distance. The two inboard ranks are back-to-back and facing outboard; the men of each outboard rank are facing inboard and are paired off with men of the adjacent inboard rank.

3. The instructor controls the drill by voice, magaphone or loudspeaker from the center or end of the formation.

(5) **Six or More Ranks.**

1. This formation is used for non-contact drill, such as basic thrust and buttstroke sequences, foot-drill, feints or practice moves, where the unit is anywhere from a platoon to a company in size. It requires more space than either of the first two formations.

2. There are six or more extended ranks at about 6-pace distance, all ranks covering and facing in the same direction.

3. The instructor controls the drill with a loudspeaker from any vantage point in front of or to the side of the formation where he can observe all hands and from which he can be heard readily.

(6) **Large Circle.**

1. This formation is employed for learning and practicing feints and practice moves—both non-contact. It is suitable for a unit from a squad to two platoons in size.

2. The formation is, as the name implies, nothing more than a single circle with each man having about 4-pace interval and facing inboard.

3. The instructor stands in the center of the circle where he can demonstrate and also conduct the drill by voice or, if the unit is quite large and hence well spread out, by loudspeaker.

e. **Bayonet Drill Commands.**—(Notes for Instructors.)

(1) **General.**—Bayonet drill commands are extremely simple and are for the most part already well-known to Marine Corps officers and non-commissioned officers. In bayonet training all sequences are first learned "by the numbers." This involves the instructor's giving one command for each movement of the sequence. When the moves of the sequence have been mastered—whether it is a thrust sequence or a feint or parry sequence—the instructor then gives but one command for the entire sequence. This command initiates the sequence, and when the men have finished it they either stop at the Guard position, Cross Over, continue a movement of Foot-Drill or do whatever else the instructor has prearranged, which in turn will depend upon what phase of bayonet training the men are in.

(2) For all moves "by the numbers" the command consists of the actual name of the move. For example, the command for a Long Thrust is simply "LONG THRUST" or "1. Long, 2. THRUST," depending upon the preference of the instructor.

(3) For all sequences the command simply describes the sequence, and, as with the commands for individual moves "by the numbers", the command can be all one command of execution, such as "VERTICAL BUTTSTROKE SEQUENCE" or divided into a preparatory command and a command of execution such as, "1. Vertical Butt Sequence, 2. MOVE." Whichever method is preferred, one method only should be used when there is more than one instructor working with a body of troops. (Platoon instructors should be consistent with each other on this point.) Abbreviations such as "THRUSTS" for the Thrust sequence are permissible and advisable.

(4) Any commands for bayonet drill not covered in this pamphlet so far will be found together with the description of the movement or sequence later on.

28. 12th Hour of Combat Conditioning.—Assemble the company in a semi-circle at the sawdust square for a demonstration of rolling with the rifle. The Combat Conditioning instructor then commences: Men, when you are in a combat area you will carry your organic weapon with you at all times as will your men. Whenever contact with the enemy is possible or imminent you will carry your rifle or carbine at the ready. Lots of times the footing will be pretty poor and you may be moving fast, as when going into position or when in the assault. So the need for being able to roll with a rifle should be apparent. Here is how it is done.

Figure 87(a).—Rolling with Rifle—Part 1.

a. **Rolling with rifle and bayonet.**—(1) Since you never know when you will trip and have to roll with your rifle, you never attempt to change your grip on your rifle but leave it exactly as it is in the Guard or High Port position. When you start to fall, immediately bend at the waist and reach down and forward with rifle, arms fairly well extended but elbows still somewhat bent. Now the rolls are exactly like they are without the rifle. The hands, rifle (right side up), and forearm help break the fall, and the roll is made either frontally or on the right shoulder, the Marine landing on his feet automatically in an On Guard position. The roll can be made on the left shoulder, but the bayonet tends to catch in the deck when this is done.

(2) Demonstrate both types of rifle roll (front and shoulder) first slow and then fast. See **Figure 87a, b, c—** The Shoulder Roll.

Figure 87(b).—Rolling with **Rifle**—Part 2.

Figure 87(c).—Rolling with Rifle—Part 3.

(3)　The company then turns to and practices the roll with rifles.　Six files of equal length on the wide edge of pit.　Men roll (front roll) across pit alternately rolling and running and reform on the other side.　Take it fairly slow at first.　Come back fast.　Roll over again slow using the shoulder roll.　Then come back fast, optional.　The company assembles again for a demonstration of foot drill.

(4)　The Instructor:　In bayonet training we try to stress good footwork from the start, and so to this end we use a system of foot-drill which is intended to help develop the bayonet fighter's ability to move and react in any direction, quickly, easily and balanced.

b.　**Foot-Drill.**—(1)　Foot-drill is an exercise given to the platoon formed for bayonet training in two ranks extended and facing each other.　Each movement has a command. Starting from the on guard position each man performs the foot movement once for each command.　He always ends up on balance in the guard position.

(2)　**Demonstrate and Explain—"ADVANCE"**— spring forward a short distance (1'-1½') from the rear foot, land easily on the forward foot and bring the rear foot up immediately to the "normal" position.

(3) **"RETIRE"**—the opposite of "advance". Spring backwards lightly from the forward foot and land easily on the rear foot, bringing the forward foot back to "normal stance" position without hesitation. It must be emphasized that these movements are **not** hops or jumps, but rather easy and quick shuffle-foot movements like those of a boxer. The feet, however, do not drag on the ground.

(4) **"LEFT"**—shift the body laterally to the left a short distance (1'-2') by springing lightly off the right foot landing easily on the left and immediately bringing up the right to its original relative position.

(5) **"RIGHT"**—exact opposite of "left". Shift body to right off left foot, landing on right and bringing left foot over instantly.

(6) **"FRONT-PASS"**—Used for closing in quickly on an opponent. Executed by stepping forward quickly with the rear foot and bringing the forward foot up in front again immediately. Note that the feet cross here whereas they did not in any of the previous foot movements. (Front-Pass amounts to two quick steps.)

(7) **"REAR-PASS"**—The reverse of "front-pass". Step backward quickly with the forward foot and bring the rear foot back to its original rear position immediately.

(8) Instructor: **These foot movements will be executed at first only one movement for each command. Later on when all hands have got them down pat, then thereafter, each movement will be executed continuously until a further command is given.** For example, at the command: "Advance", you will advance continuously until another command is given. **This applies to all movements** except "Whirl". You will whirl but once for each command and immediately resume whichever foot movement you were doing directly before." (Demonstrate.)

(9) As you get proficient in this foot work, the instructors drilling you will spring the command "Thrusts" into the middle of it at which time you will immediately go into the thrust sequence of long and short thrusts we taught you and then come to high port, cross over, whirl and stand fast on guard. Get the habit of yelling when you come on guard and when you whirl. When the command "Vertical Buttstrokes" comes, go right into that sequence without hesitation and finish up as before. He may also give "Thrusts and Horizontal Buttstrokes" or "Vertical Buttstrokes and Thrusts" which means combine the two sequences and finish up by high port and cross over.

(10) Demonstrate each of the above sequences and combinations worked into foot-drill. Then turn to on foot drill by platoons, practicing progressively single movements of foot-drill, then continuous movement and finally, mixing in thrust and butt-stroke sequences.

(11) Allow about 10 minutes at the end of the hour for the men to pair off and practice straight parries with each other, scabbards on.

(12) End up by duck-waddling a distance of seventy-five to one hundred yards, holding rifle straight out to the front.

29. 13th Hour of Combat Conditioning Program.—Begin hour by rolling the company across sawdust pit a few times with rifles, bayonets and scabbards fixed. Then assemble in a circle.

a. **Review.**—The Combat Conditioning instructor will give a rapid yet complete review of all previous bayonet work covered to date (stance, grip, foot-drill, whirl, jumping, thrusts, and straight parries) using other Combat Conditioning Section instructors to demonstrate. He will clear up any questions that may occur, but will not spend too much time on the review.

b. **Practice Rolling and Jumping with Rifle and Bayonet.**
(Instructor's Note.)

(1) The company will break up into platoons for a rotating workout as follows:

1st Platoon—Hurdling sawdust-filled ditch, N end of bayonet course—3-4 minutes.

2d Platoon—Hand vaulting the Abdominal Rise Rail—3-4 minutes.

3d Platoon—Rolling with Rifle in Sawdust Square (Stay clear of Abdominal Rise Rail)—3-4 minutes.

Platoon will rotate twice and finish up. Total time—about 10-12 minutes.

(2) Then the company will turn to by platoons on reviewing all bayonet work to date. It is intended that each platoon be formed into two ranks and the platoon instructor supervising give the men foot and sequence movements by command. Include all the foot-drill movements and separate and/or combined sequences. (Reference: Section 7 28(b), p. 224.) Do not go through any movements "by the numbers" (i.e., Long Thrust or Withdraw) for **once learned, these movements must come smoothly and instinctively.** Therefore only the initial commands will be given for sequence moves. The normal commands will be given for foot-drill, each movement (whirl excepted) being executed continuously until superceded by another command.

(3) It is permissible to allow candidates to run the drill after the platoon instructors have it well started. However, platoon instructors or candidates should not overlap or repeat instructions which the Combat Conditioning Section has just given. (Allow about 10 minutes for the above review.)

The platoon instructors then resume charge and have the ranks close in, the men pairing off and reviewing straight parries left and right. One man will "stand fast" (on guard, motionless) while his partner practices straight parries and thrusts on him from various distances. The man standing fast will hold his piece firmly, offering some resistance to the parry; the men parrying will thrust his partner very lightly. Scabbards will be on at all times. Each man has his turn at the parry and thrust.

c. **Hand Signals.**—(1) **Combat Conditioning Instructor:** As we have told you, bayonet training is progressive in nature and a great deal of it requires men working against each other in pairs. We have one exercise for men working in pairs used for the developing of speed, coordination and quick reaction. This is the "Hand Signals Exercise" in which one man, unarmed, offers himself as a target for the second man, who has the rifle and bayonet, scabbard fixed. The unarmed man is the signal-caller, calls the other on guard by this signal (demonstrate) and places himself in front of the armed man as a target.

(2) **Positions.**—There are two simple sequences of movements used, the **thrust sequence** and the **butt sequence.** The unarmed man denotes the sequence to be employed by the relation in which he places himself to his opponent's bayonet. To call for the **thrust sequence** the signal-caller places himself directly in front of his opponent so that his opponent's bayonet tip touches his chest. See Figure 88a. (Demonstrate.) To call for the **butt sequence** he would place himself slightly to the right front of his opponent so that the blade touches the side of his right shoulder. (Demonstrate.) Having called his opponent on guard and having placed himself before his opponent correctly the signal-caller then gives hand signals, one for each movement of the prescribed sequence of moves. Each time he gives a hand signal he moves quickly to the rear, escaping the blow aimed at him. The instant a signal is given the armed man strikes at the signal-caller, executing the movement prescribed by the signal and the sequence. After each signal and corresponding blow the signal-caller quickly replaces himself close to and in front of his opponent ready to give the next signal.

Figure 88(a).—Hand Signals—Thrusts—Part 1.

(3) **Thrust Sequence—SIGNALS.**—(Demonstrate the signals only—no opponent yet.)

(4) **Long Thrust.**—Right hand, fingers spread, placed palm against chest, throat or stomach. As soon as palm touches chest, bayonet man may make his move, trying to thrust the signal-caller's signal hand wherever it is placed. See Figure 88b. Withdrawal is fast and automatic. Bayonet man will keep his piece back at position of short guard. Signal-caller comes up to him and places bayonet point against his chest. (See Figure 88c.)

Figure 88(b).—Hand Signals—Thrusts—Part 2.

Figure 88(c).—Hand Signals—Thrusts—Part 3.

229

(5) **Short Thrust.**—Right fist against chest or stomach. Bayonet man will strike when fist touches signal-caller's chest. Withdraw automatically. See Figure 88d.

(6) **Butt Sequence—Signals.**—(Show signals—don't demonstrate the moves yet.)

(7) **On Guard.**—Right fist forward, forearm horizontal, elbow at hip. See Figure 89a.

(8) **Vertical Buttstroke.**—Raise the right fist up from Guard position in a swift, uppercut motion. See Figure 89b.

Figure 88(d).—Hand Signals—Thrusts—Part 4.

Figure 89(a).—Hand Signals—Buttstrokes—Part 1.

(9) **Smash.**—Right arm raised to the front, elbow bent, fist doubled. Jab three or four times with fist towards your opponent. See Figure 89c.

(10) **Slash.**—Starting from position of the right hand (fingers extended and joined and as an extension of wrist and forearm) touching the junction of left shoulder and neck, "cutting edge" of hand to front, make a quick diagonal slashing movement downward and to the right. This slashing move with the hand is the "go" signal for the bayonet man. See Figures 89d, 89e.

Figure 89(b).—Hand Signals—Buttstrokes—Part 2.

Figure 89(c).—Hand Signals—Buttstrokes—Part 3.

232

R.D. 4443

Figure 89(d).—Hand Signals—Buttstrokes—Part 4.

Figure 89(e).—Hand Signals—Buttstrokes—Part 5.

(11) **Overhand.**—Starting with right fist and arm to the front, make a sharp overhand "hook" movement. See Figure 89f.

(12) **Horizontal Buttstroke.**—Start with right fist and arm slightly higher than guard position. "Go" signal is the execution of a sharp, horizontal, right hook. For the Horizontal Buttstroke sequence the other signals employed are identical to those of the Vertical Butt Sequence.

R.D. 4443

Figure 89(f).—Hand Signals—Buttstrokes—Part 6.

(13)　Now let's see how this actually works with two men. First the **Thrust Sequence.** (Combat Conditioning Section instructors demonstrate.) Bayonet fighter called on guard; signal-caller comes right up to him till his chest touches the bayonet tip. As soon as his hand strikes his chest for the **Long Thrust** signal, the bayonet fighter makes his move and the "target" back-pedals to the rear. Withdrawal is automatic, bringing bayonet man to the position of short guard. Signal-caller immediately "recovers"—that is, he comes up to the blade just as before, letting it touch his solar-plexus this time. Then the Short Thrust.

(14) Now for the Vertical Butt Stroke Series. Called on guard as before and signal-caller's right shoulder touches flat of blade. This is intended to show that butt strokes are natural when an opponent is "inside" your blade. There's the vertical butt stroke aimed for the crotch, stomach, and jaw! Notice that the signal-caller "recovered" and placed his jaw within six (6) inches of the rifle butt, now in position for the smash, and his right side is towards the man with the rifle. That is the way that you are going to do it! You've got to move fast. This is the only way that you will get any good out of it. It's give and take all the way!

(15) There's the smash — two jabbing motions by the bayonet man. Notice how he extended his arms and how the signal-caller got away from the butt. After the smash, come up again close to the butt. Then the slash. Recover, coming right in front of the bayonet man again a foot or two away. Upon giving your "overhand" signal move back rapidly quite a distance, because after the bayonet fighter executes the overhand smash, he moves forward, coming "on guard" automatically and vigorously.

(16) Now the men swap over. They'll show you the sequences again.

(17) Demonstrated again by the Combat Conditioning Section instructors with bare blade and no punches pulled.

(18) You notice that each man has his chance with the rifle and bayonet. As I said before, the only way either man gets any good out of this exercise is to start each movement close to each other as we have prescribed and for the bayonet man to hit hard with everything he has. After all, the man who gives the signals has the advantage because he knows when he is going to give the signal and can move back the instant he does, whereas the bayonet man has to see the signal and then react. So the signal-caller, if he moves fast, should always be able to avoid being hit. If he does get hit once, he will move faster the next time. We don't ever want to see the bayonet man pull a punch! If he does this, he is letting both himself and his partner down because neither will benefit from the practice. Remember that turn about is fair play, and you had both better be hard with each other. One more thing—the good of the exercises is in developing speed, coordination, and reaction by executing of prearranged blows at a live target upon signal. Therefore, don't try to make a close order drill game out of it and mix the signals up indiscriminately. We don't want that at all! Stick to the prescribed sequences bearing in mind that this is only one means to an end: to make you capable, bayonet fighters able to fight on your own, taking instant advantage of any opening in the best way possible.

(19) Turn to on hand signals in platoon areas, working in pairs. Finish up the hour on this.

236

30. 14th Hour of Combat Conditioning.—a. **Orientation.**—
(Note for Instructors.)

(1)   If the candidates have practiced hard for about
ten or fifteen minutes during the previous hour on Hand
Signals, working in pairs, and also if it appears that there will
be thirty minutes or more left in the fourteenth hour, then
run a **Wheelbarrow-Race** between platoons in the sawdust pit.

(2)   Then the company assembles for work on Shift
Parries. Combat Conditioning Section Instructor: Now so
far, you have learned many fundamental moves and techniques
in bayonet fighting including stance, grip, footwork, jumping
and vaulting, thrusts, butt strokes, a simple slash, and straight
parries. We have stressed balance, speed, accuracy, reaction,
and aggressiveness. These are the primary fundamentals that
should be taught to beginners with the bayonet. You are
fairly proficient in these fundamentals because of the work
you have had here and because of your bayonet work in recruit
training.

(3)   There are a few more fundamentals to learn
and after that some refinements which will help you become
a much better bayonet fighter than you are now, especially
if you practice diligently. The next thing that we **are going**
to take up is the so-called shift parry.

b.   **The Shift Parry.**—The shift parry is a very potent
parry that can be used counteroffensively as well as offensively. It involves stepping quickly to one side and forward,
parrying your opponent's blade to the opposite side and down,
and coming into him with your blade or butt. Here is how it
works. First, the **shift parry left.** The Combat Conditioning
Section Instructors will demonstrate—first normal speed and
then slowly, "by the numbers."

Figure 90(a).—Shift Parry Left—Part 1.

(1) **The Shift Parry Left.**—Position: bayonet fighters facing each other, bayonet tips about six (6) inches to one foot apart and directly in line with each other.

(2) **As Counter to Enemy's Thrust.**—The enemy bayonet fighter starts a long or short thrust towards you. Here it is with the long thrust first.

1. Keeping your eyes on his blade and keeping your own blade slightly higher than and right of his, move quickly and easily to the right and slightly forward (right foot first, followed by left). As you move, start to engage his bayonet with the flat, left side of yours, not making contact until your blade crosses his on top "at an angle," thus minimizing chances of your missing his blade. Notice that even if you miss his blade you have shifted your body to the side, out of the way of his thrust.

2. As you make contact with his blade, parry it sharply down and slightly to the left with your blade. You have held your rifle roughly horizontal and sling down and forward. Now you whip your left hand (on the front hand guard) smartly down and across to the left and raise up smartly a few inches your right hand (on the small of the stock). This blow will parry his blade down and somewhat to the left. It will unbalance him and also let you inside his blade and where he can't get at you with his butt but where his vitals are exposed to you. See Figure 90a.

3. Without losing a fraction of a second, rotate your rifle slightly counter-clockwise without changing your hands and bring your blade (cutting edge first) quickly up from his bayonet and along his rifle towards his throat, slashing his hand and biceps on the way. Use either a series of quick, choppy slashes or make it all one big sweeping slash. Figure 90b. This slashing of the hand and arm is secondary and will be used only whenever there is good opportunity and time to execute it. The **throat** is the primary objective! Slash it vigorously with the tip or cutting edge of your blade. See Figure 90c.

Figure 90(b).—Shift Parry Left—Part 2.

Figure 90(c).—Shift Parry Left—Part 3.

4. From here you can follow through in either of two ways: by drawing your rifle and bayonet back and thrusting into his kidney—Figure 90d—or by butt-stroking him in the side or on the head. Figure 90e.

(3) Instructor's Note: The CC Section Instructors will demonstrate the move once more slowly, explaining it in detail as they do. They will show also how if the enemy was coming fast—the slash could be eliminated and a butt-stroke used right after the parry. (Demonstrate once fast; then once, slow.)

(4)   Instructor explains and demonstrates (against a **short thrust**) that when the enemy uses a short thrust, the shift parry left can be made more diagonally or horizontally than vertically. This is done simply by engaging your enemy's bayonet from the left side rather than the top and warding it smartly to the left and slightly down by pulling your left hand (on the front hand guard) smartly to the left and pushing your right hand (on the small of the stock) slightly to the right and slightly up. As the blunt edge of your blade makes contact with his, your blade should be pointing up at an angle of about 15°-20° and the plane of the rifle butt will be "diagonal" whereas before it was almost horizontal. More "reach" on your part will be necessary.

Figure 90(d).—Shift Parry Left—Part 4.

Figure 90(e).—Shift Parry Left—Part 5.

(5) **Used Offensively.**—Position is same as before. Enemy does not execute thrust, however, but "stands fast". (On Guard, firm but motionless.) This time you take the initiative as follows:

1. Same as before except move less to the right and more to the front (otherwise you won't be able to reach him). Your footwork amounts to a front-pass, closing the distance. You must reach out more than before, too.

2. Same, except hold your butt slightly lower than before and make your parry more to the left and less downward, even more so than as you did against the short thrust.

3. Same.

4. Same. You may not be able to reach him with your butt as easily as with your blade.

Next comes the counterpart to the shift parry left.

(6) **The Shift Parry Right.**—This movement is also used both aggressively and counteroffensively and involves moving the body forward and to the left and parrying the enemy's blade to the right.

242

Figure 91(a).—Shift Parry Right—Part 1.

(7) Used Counteroffensively—**Same Position.**— Fighters facing each other, bayonet tips in line and about six inches to one foot apart. Your enemy starts a thrust towards you. You act and counter by:

1. Keeping your eyes on his blade and keeping your own blade slightly higher than and left of his, move quickly to the left and slightly forward (left foot first, followed by right). As you move, start to engage his bayonet from the left with the flat, left side of your blade, not making contact until your blade will cross his "at an angle", thus minimizing the chances of your missing his blade. This parry is more awkward and unnatural to make than the shift parry left. Sometimes it is found safer to engage your enemy's blade from its side **with the cutting edge of your blade.** Notice that as in the shift parry left, you have shifted your body to the side and out of the way of his thrust.

2. As you make contact with his blade, parry it sharply to the right and down with your blade. This you do by holding your rifle (roughly horizontal, sling towards your right) across your right front and pushing to the left and down with your left hand on the front hand guard and pulling back your right hand, on the small of the stock, sharply towards you. This will deflect his thrust to the right and down, unbalancing him at the same time. See Figure 91a.

243

It will also leave you inside of his blade with his vitals exposed. Notice, however, that here, as contrasted to your position on the shift-parry left, your are vulnerable for a stroke from his butt. Also if you try to slash back along his rifle towards his throat with the half-sharpened edge of your bayonet he can block the movement easily by simply raising his butt up— so that his rifle is vertical, muzzle down—leaving his blade down. He can block your butt stroke in the same manner. Therefore, immediately after making your parry, execute 3.

Figure 91(b).—Shift Parry Right—Part 2.

3. Bring your blade directly to your enemy's throat and either slash it back and forth with the tip of your bayonet or thrust the blade into the base of his throat. See Figure 91b. In combat you may have most of the non-cutting edge of your blade, battle-sharpened with a file. With a blade like this, one sweeping back-slash would be sufficient.

(Instructor's Note.)

(8) Demonstrate the movement once, fast, and twice, slow with explanations. Then demonstrate the Shift Parry Right against the short thrust, explaining why you must parry more to the side than down and also that you must employ more arm reach than before.

(9) **The Shift Parry Right.**—Can be used **offensively** when your enemy does not thrust. It will be done in the same manner just described except that your movement should

be much more forward and less to the left and your parry much more to the right and less down. (Demonstrate a couple of times.) Answer any questions, then turn to by platoons on shift parries. Men will be paired off and working from a correct **position** as described. Scabbards will be fixed at all times. **Candidates and instructors must be sure that the scabbards are always on and are intact—allowing no cutting steel to protrude. This will be the responsibility of all instructors and candidates alike whenever candidates work against each other with the bayonet.**

(10)   Leave 10 minutes at the end of the hour for running the bayonet course.

(11)   **Bayonet Course.**—Refer to Figures 103, 103a, 103b, 103c, 103d. A CC Section instructor will first lead the men through the course, orienting them. Then the company will break up into four equal files back of each foxhole and will run through the course with bare bayonets once. In so far as possible there will be instructors at each target to see that the course is run properly and to make corrections. The course will be run as prescribed in Section 7, Paragraph 35a with the exception that at the last target the man will make a long thrust instead of a feint. (These latter haven't been taught yet.)

31.   Fifteenth Hour of C. C. Program.—(Note for Instructors.)—1st Half of Company (alphabetically)—15th Hour of Course.

2d Half of Company (alphabetically)—16th Hour of Course.

Company lined up in six files at S. edge of sawdust square with rifles, bayonets and scabbards fixed. Roll with rifles across the pit, duckwaddle back around, roll across again and roll back. Then the company will split up into two groups, the first half (alphabetically) going to one Combat Conditioning Section instructor in one area for work on Shift Parries and the second half (alphabetically) going to a second Combat Conditioning Section instructor for work on practice movements, parries, guards, and feints.

a.   **Shift Parries.**—(1)   **Shift Parry, Right and Left.** (Refer to Shift Parries, Section 7, Paragraph 30b.)

First half of company assembled in a circle. The C. C. Section instructor will first demonstrate and explain as a review the Left and Right Shift Parries as used both offensively and counteroffensively. Then he will proceed to demonstrate, explain, and discuss the variations of the Shift Parry one by one. All but one of these variations can be worked to the left only in actual practice.

(2)   **The Deck Parry.**—This is used when your opponent comes thrusting towards you **with a rush. This is the only variation that is practicable to the right as well as to the left.**

(3) **Deck Parry Left.**—1. Shift body to right and engage his blade from top and right with the left, flat side of your blade.

2. Parry his blade sharply down and force it all the way to the deck with the left, flat side of your bayonet. His blade will probably stick in the deck or it will unbalance him so that he will pile up against his own rifle butt.

3. Buttstroke him in the side or head as he comes past you or else trip him and then stick him while he is sprawled on the deck.

(4) **Deck Parry Right.**—1. Shift your body to the left with a left step and engage his bayonet from the top and left with either the cutting edge of your blade or with its left, flat side, whichever you can work better. The former is probably more reliable.

2. Same as with Deck Parry Left.

3. Stick him in the throat as he goes by or trip him and stick him in a vital spot when he lands.

b. **Controlled Parries.**—(Instructors, refer to Bayonet Drill Formations, Section 7, Paragraph 27d, p. 219.)

(1) In a moment we are going to have a session of controlled parries, which is a system for teaching parries to a number of bayonet students by controlled, contact work. You will be lined up in four equal ranks at double-arms' interval and about 4-pace distance, covering in file. The first and third ranks will then about-face, facing the second and fourth ranks, respectively. Thus each man will automatically be paired off with a partner and there will be two inboard ranks, facing out, and two outboard ranks, facing in.

(2) Now when you come "on guard" we want you to shift around a bit, if necessary, so that your bayonet tip is exactly in line with your partner's and about six (6) inches to a foot apart at the start of each move. This is important, because if you "set up" a parry for your buddy he is going to get little or no benefit out of executing it, nor are you either. You won't be able to see just how that parry must be made in order to be effective. So make each other work hard all of the time!

(3) We will then practice the shift parries and their variations one by one as we learn them. First it will be controlled. Later on you will practice them uncontrolled by yourselves. For now, upon my command one rank will make a Short or Long Thrust, as I indicate, and the opposite rank of men will make the parry and follow through as I prescribe. For example I may say, "Inboard ranks, Long Thrust—outboard ranks, Shift Parry Left, Slash and Thrust. 1. Stand by, 2. MOVE! You will both move on the command "Move!" Then recover, coming back to your original positions and I will have the outboard ranks thrust this time and the inboard ranks parry upon command. We expect the ranks executing the

thrust to actually make hard thrusts right at the opposite ranks. **I may vary the procedure and make you use the shift parries and variations offensively by eliminating the thrust and having one rank just "stand fast,"** that is, be rigidly on guard while the other ranks come in, shift parrying offensively. Varying the procedure like this will help you gauge distance and also give you practice in using the parries under a variety of conditions.

(Instructor's Notes.)

(4) The instructor then carries the Candidates controlled through the Shift and Deck Parries, Right and Left, using combinations of the long thrust, short thrust or stand fast and any follow-through of the following:

Shift Parry Follow-Throughs

LEFT		RIGHT	
SHIFT PARRY	DECK PARRY	SHIFT PARRY	DECK PARRY
1. **Slash** (hand, arm and **Thrust** (kidney)	Same	1. **Slash or Thrust** (Throat)	Same
2. **Slash** (hand, arm & throat) **and Butt‑stroke** (Side of head)	Same	2. None	**Trip and Thrust** Fallen Opponent
3. **Buttstroke Side**	Same		
4. **Buttstroke Head**	Same		
5. None	**Trip and Thrust** Fallen Opponent		

These follow-throughs for each move are reviewed by the instructor just prior to the actual practice. (In the above list the commands for each follow-through appear in bold face.) Platoon instructors will supervise and assist closely.

(5) The practice will continue for about five to fifteen minutes and then the instructor will make this announcement:

By now you should be getting the feel of the shift parries and their simulated follow-throughs. Now in order to speed you up, we're going to make the man making the thrust, thrust even harder than before, right for your throat or middle, but this time as soon as you have engaged him and started your parry—but not before!—we're going to have him try and block your follow-through with his rifle or bayonet. Any questions on that? The practice continues along this new vein for a few minutes.

c. **Shift Parry Variations.**—(Instructor's Notes.)

Next the instructor assembles the unit in a circle and demonstrates and explains the other variations to the Shift Parry: the Double Parry, the Disengage, and the Miss. Controlled practice is then resumed in the original formation.

(1) **Double Parry.**—To be used when you don't parry his blade hard enough to create an opening at first. Practical only to the left because the extra maneuver would allow him time enough to buttstroke you if you worked it to the right.

1. Shift body to right and engage his blade from top and right.

2. Parry his blade down and to the left. You didn't hit it hard enough.

3. Parry his blade down and left again hard. This should do it.

4. Follow through in any of follow-throughs numbers 1. to 4. for Shift Parry Left shown under Paragraph b (4).

(2) **Disengage.**—To use if your opponent has parried your blade down and has pinned it there as you moved to parry his. Also practicable to the left only, and rather tricky at that.

1. Instead of trying to pull up against his blade bearing down on yours, quickly jerk your blade back and out from under and bring it down and left hard on his blade thus parrying him.

2. Follow through quickly with any of follow-throughs 1. to 4. for Shift Parry Left.

3. As an alternative to this situation you can raise your butt to protect your body and simultaneously slash up into his knees, thighs or crotch with your blade.

(3) **Miss.**—To use in case you attempted a Shift Parry Left and missed his blade. Won't work for Shift Parry Right. (You would close instead of trying to parry or you might have to block a butt stroke if he had started one.)

1. Before he can swing his blade towards you, draw your blade back and come back quickly and hard on top of his blade, parrying it down and to the left.

2. Follow through quickly with any of follow-throughs 1. to 4. for Shift Parry Left.

The instructor demonstrates these three moves separately, first fast (one time) and then twice, slow, with explanation.

The men then turn to and practice these and the previous Parry moves, controlled as before, for about 15 minutes. Then let the Candidates pair off in platoon areas and practice these parries with each other uncontrolled for the remainder of the hour. Platoon instructors stay with their own platoons and make corrections.

d. **Bayonet Course.**—At the end of the last (16th) hour both halves of the company will run the entire bayonet course, each man going through twice, the first time medium speed and the second time fast. (10-15 minutes). For details of the bayonet course see Section 7, Paragraph 35a, p. 287.

1st Half of Company (Alphabetically)—16th Hour of Combat Conditioning Program. 2d Half of Company (Alphabetically)—15th Hour of Combat Conditioning Program.

32. 16th Hour of Combat Conditioning Program.—The men are assembled and seated in a circle for Practice Exercises, Feints, Foot-Drill, and Square and Squat Guards and Parries.

a. **Practice Moves.**—Combat Conditioning Section Instructor: This hour we are going to work on a few refinements of bayonet training. We will consider first a few practice moves that have little practical use in fighting but are excellent for use in the progressive bayonet training of a Marine in improving his coordination and bolstering his confidence in his ability to handle his rifle and bayonet. Later we will learn some feints and some simple parries which can be used effectively in actual bayonet fighting. We will learn and practice the movements controlled at first and then when you have them down fairly well, you will pair off and practice in pairs uncontrolled. For part of the controlled phase we will include foot-drill in the commands.

First of all, let's consider the practice moves I spoke of. Now from the position of **On Guard** you can face quickly to the rear and meet an imaginary enemy coming from that direction by executing the Reverse. Demonstrate and explain.

(1) **Reverse.**—1. Bring the front hand guard up and to the rear with your left hand at the same time turning your face and body to the right and pushing to the left with your right hand on the small of the stock. Your feet do not move except to pivot clockwise on their respective balls.

2. Let go with both hands when the left is approximately over the right, let the rifle spin vertically in mid-air (muzzle going to right, butt to left), and catch it with your right hand by the front hand guard and your left hand on the small of the stock. You are now in a position of Reverse Guard facing to your original rear. See Figure 92.

3. Shift your feet slightly to improve your balance if necessary. You may also shift your grip slightly if necessary. "To Reverse" from this position, you simply spin the rifle back (counter-clockwise from your viewpoint), turn your body back to the left and catch the rifle in the normal position of On Guard. It is very doubtful if the Reverse would ever be used in actual bayonet fighting by anyone other than an expert to meet a sudden attack from the rear. This is because under the strain of the moment you might drop the rifle or your enemy might knock it from your hands. It is good to use for practicing, however, and will improve your manipulation of rifle and bayonet. Next is the "change over" movement.

Figure 92.—Reverse Guard.

Figure 93.—Change Over.

(2) **Change Over.**—This practice movement goes hand-in-hand with the Reverse. It allows you to shift your guard from a "reversed" guard position to a "normal" **On Guard** position without turning away from the enemy you are facing. The movement also gains a little distance for you as you do it, to minimize his chances of getting to you as you execute the move. Assume you are already in a Reverse Guard position.

       1. Step back with the leading foot (in this case the right), and as you do, push forward with your left hand (on the small of the stock) and bring the rifle butt across your body from the left side to the right side. Let go of your right hand's grip on the front hand guard.

2. Let go of the small of the stock with your left hand and catch it in your right. Catch the front hand guard with your left hand. You are now in the "normal" **On Guard** position. See Figure 93.

3. The Change Over can be executed from the normal, on guard position. Simply step to the rear again with the leading foot (this time the left foot) meanwhile passing the butt in front of your body from right to left and changing hands on the small of the stock and the front hand guard. You end up in a reverse guard position.

In order to avoid confusing the **Reverse** and the **Change Over** remember this: On the Reverse you don't change your feet but you do face in a new direction. On the Change Over you do change your feet (by stepping to the Rear with the leading foot) but you do not face in a new direction.

The Change Over is purely a practice move that you wouldn't rely on in bayonet combat unless you were expert and except under rather extraordinary conditions where you had executed a reverse and wanted to get back to your normal guard position—which is of course easiest to fight from. You might actually have a use for the change over in a bayonet fight. If your left hand were so badly cut that you couldn't control your bayonet you might Change Over and cradle the rifle butt tightly under your left arm and carry on as best you could from there. Your other alternative would be to cradle your front hand guard or front part of the stock in the crook of your left elbow and to use your right hand at the small of the stock to control your rifle.

There is a movement, which you already know, which can be worked in with the Reverse and Change Over to keep you on your toes and that is the Reversed Whirl.

(3) **Reversed Whirl.**—To whirl from the Reverse guard position simply snap the right hand (with the front hand guard) up to your right shoulder, pivot to the **right-about** on the ball of your leading (right) foot and snap the blade back to the Reverse Guard position. The movement is fast, unified and continuous.

Having demonstrated each of these three movements two or three times form the detail in either two ranks facing each other and separated by about 15 yards or else a large circle with the entire detail. The instructor will then give the candidates a short period of practice in the movements they have just seen demonstrated taking it slowly at first. First give them the Reverse and Change Over until they are fairly proficient with them both "normally" and "reversed." Then give them a little practice whirling with the rifle at Reverse Guard. Explain that they will now receive foot-drill interspersed with new movements. After each Reverse, Change Over or Whirl they will resume the foot movement they were doing directly before. The instructor's commands might now run something like this: On guard, Advance, Right, Retire, Left, Front Pass, Whirl, Retire, Reverse, Whirl, Change Over, Rear Pass, etc.

b. **Feints.**—The unit assembles for a demonstration and explanation of the three feints—Front-Pass-and-Throw, Gain-Point-High-Slash-Low, and Gain-Point-Low-Slash-High. CC Section Instructor: Just as a good boxer must be able at times to feint his opponent into an opening, so a bayonet fighter may find it necessary to do the same thing. If his opponent appears to have a good defense he should feint him off guard and then close in, instead of rushing in blindly from the start. Thus parries and feints supplement each other. Each are important, Parries are perhaps more fundamental and are therefore taught first. Both should be learned and practiced.

(1) **Front-Pass-and-Throw.**—This is a feint that is used when still approaching an enemy bayonet fighter. It is a feint at throwing your rifle, bayonet first, at him and, is intended to worry and unbalance him. This feint is not used when your enemy is close enough to reach you or knock the rifle out of your hands. Executed as follows, usually while running or "front-passing" towards the enemy:

1. Step forward with the right foot and at the same time release your grip on the front hand guard with your left hand and shoot the rifle and bayonet out horizontally in the direction of your enemy's throat. Be sure and hold on strongly with your right hand to the small of the stock. Support the rifle with your right forearm on the comb of the stock if necessary. See Figure 94.

Figure 94.—Front-Pass and Throw.

2. Step forward vigorously with the left foot and catch the front hand guard in your left hand. End up balanced and ready for action in the position of **On Guard.** If necessary you can jump forward slightly with your right foot as you bring your left up. You should be close enough to your enemy to engage him now.

3. The "Front-Pass-and-Throw" or "Throw-Point" as it is sometimes called can be used to thrust from a distance an unarmed enemy who is running backwards away from you. This would probably be the only case you would actually thrust a man with a Front-Pass-and-Throw or "Throw-Point" as this one-armed thrust is often called, because unless your enemy is off his guard and unless you have a very strong arm, there is too much chance of your dropping the rifle or of his knocking it from your hands.

(2) **Gain-Point-High-Slash-Low.**—This is a basic feint which can be used as it is or varied at will. Speed and accuracy, which come from practice, are essential.

R.D. 4443

Figure 95(a).—Gain-Point-High-Slash-Low—Part 1.

Position: Facing your opponent, bayonet blades in line
and about six inches to one foot, tip-to-tip. Notice that from
your present position you cannot reach out or slash or thrust
any part of his body proper or his legs. See Figure 95a. Demonstrate the following movement once fast and then slow
with description and explanation.

1. Flick the tip of your bayonet up a couple
of inches and raise your butt sharply as high as your face.
Simultaneously bring your right foot up to touch your left
and plant it on the deck. This will put you in a position where
you can reach him with your blade. (You "gain" reach.) Your
enemy will be watching your bayonet and will not notice your
foot come up. He will probably instinctively raise his blade
some, enough to let you get underneath his guard. Notice that
you did not actually raise your blade very high at all but just
enough to fool your enemy.

2. Step forward and slightly to the right with
your left foot, bending your left knee. See Figure 95b. Reach
out and slash your enemy across the thighs with a fast movement. See Figure 95c.

3. Rear Pass to the rear quickly.

Figure 95(b).—Gain-Point-High-Slash-Low—Part 2.

Figure 95(c).—Gain-Point-High-Slash-Low—Part 3.

As you can see, this move must be executed very quickly and accurately in order that you can get inside his guard and do the damage without getting hurt yourself. But with a bit of effort and practice you can develop a very effective feint out of it. There are variations to what you may do, depending to some extent upon your enemy's reaction to your feint. If he does not move his blade high enough or at all you may have to execute a quick shift parry left. Or you may find it easier to move your right foot up after your left and thrust his midsection or throat. Naturally if you get to a vital spot on your slash or thrust you would stay in and finish your enemy off instead of rear-passing. Remember that!

The third basic feint is the counterpart of the second feint.

Figure 96(a).—Gain-Point-Low-Slash-High—Part 1.

Figure 96(b).—Gain-Point-Low-Slash-High—Part 2.

(3) **Gain-Point-Low-Slash-High.**—1. Drop your bayonet tip sharply about six inches or a foot and raise your butt a couple of inches at the same time, thus increasing the low "point". Simultaneously bring your right foot up to your left and plant it on the deck. As before, your enemy will be watching your blade and not your feet and will probably drop his blade to protect himself. You will have "gained" reach in the meantime. See Figure 96a.

2. Quickly step forward and slightly to the right with your left foot and reach out and slash his throat with your bayonet tip. See Figure 96b. The slash is made by pushing the left hand smartly to the right and jerking the right hand a few inches to the left. The bayonet is "flat" and nearly horizontal.

3. Rear-Pass to the rear quickly.

As before, there are variations depending upon his reaction and also upon your balance and reach. You may find it easier to step off forward and to the right with your right foot. You may have to execute a shift parry left and follow through if he does not drop his blade enough. It may be that all you can do is slash and disable his hand. This, of course, is much better than nothing because it will weaken his defense considerably. **Bear in mind, however, that there is no time for fencing, so bore in and finish him off as soon as possible.**

Naturally you wouldn't rear-pass if you got him in a vital spot. For "dry" practice (where there is no opponent) you will execute the rear-pass as part of the move.

(4) Instructor's Note. — Having demonstrated these three basic feints and the potential variations to the satisfaction of the candidates, the instructor will give the candidates practice in them controlled as before, taking it slowly at first and then working them in with foot-drill and the other moves. The formation will be the circle again.

(5) The instructor's commands for the feints will be "Front-Pass-and-Throw; Gain-Point-High-Slash-Low; and Gain-Point-Low-Slash-High" and the candidates will execute the prescribed movement once for each command and will then continue the foot movement (if any) that they were doing immediately before. The instructor can give "Front-Pass-and-Throw-Gain-Point-Slash-High" and the candidates will execute first the "Throw-point" and then the other prescribed feint right after it. The instructor should explain this command and sequence before using it. (About 10 minutes.)

When the candidates are getting along fairly well on these moves, assemble for a demonstration of the final two movements.

c. **Defensive Positions and Parries.**—We now have two defensive parries that can be quite useful under certain circumstances. These are the square parry and the squat parry. First of all the guard positions corresponding to the parries.

Figure 97(a).—Square Guard and Thrust Parry—Part 1.

(1) **The Square Guard.**—Demonstrate a couple of times.

1. From a position of On Guard, pivot on the ball of your right foot and **step back** with your left foot to a position 1½′ to 2′ to the left of your right foot.

2. Simultaneously turn your body to face the front and raise the rifle up to a horizontal position, sling up, across your chest. Your hands should be opposite your respective shoulders. See Figure 97a. To go back to "On Guard" from "Square Guard" simply pivot on the ball of the **left** foot and **step to the rear** with the right, bringing the rifle down to On Guard position.

3. The Square Guard is not ordinarily used as a primary position in bayonet combat. It is useful in peace time in controlling mobs and crowds. In combat it can be used as a basis for parrying when you are attacked suddenly from close quarters and don't have time for other types of parries. You can parry a thrust or block a butt stroke from the square guard position.

(2) **Parries from the Square Guard.**—

(a) **Against a Thrust.**—

1. Pull your body to the rear, extend your arms to the front and come down hard on the top of his bayonet, knocking it as low as possible. See Figure 97b.

2. Either step around his blade and come up hard to his throat and jaw with your rifle stock, driving straight out from your shoulders or just pin his bayonet to the deck with a foot and come in as before with a hard blow to the throat or jaw. If the move is worked correctly and with sufficient speed your opponent will be unable to slash up with his bayonet. See Figure 97c.

Figure 97(b).—Square Guard and Thrust Parry—Part 2.

R.D. 4443

Figure 97(c).—Square Guard and Thrust Parry—Part 3.

(b) **To Block a Buttstroke.**—Either a horizontal or a vertical buttstroke can be blocked from the square guard.

1. Extend your rifle straight out across the path of his buttstroke and block it. Try to catch the buttstroke before it gets its momentum.

2. Quickly force your opponent back by pushing on his rifle with yours and attempt to kick or knee him in the crotch.

Finally we have the Squat Guard and the Squat Parry. For initial practice, the Squat Guard position is assumed as follows:

(3) **Squat Guard.**—1. From position of High Port or On Guard drop down to the right knee, crouching low, eyes on opponent.

2. Simultaneously and without changing the position of your hands, bring the rifle to a vertical position about one foot squarely in front of your body with the butt on the deck, sling to the front, and bayonet pointing straight up or slightly to the right.

The Squat Guard is a practice position from which the Squat Parry can be executed.

R.D. 4443

Figure 98.—Squat Guard, Showing the Squat Parry.

(4) **The Squat Parry.**—This will be used against a Thrust or Butt Smash.

1. Keep your eyes on your enemy's blade or butt. Move your left hand sharply to the left or right (most easily and less dangerously done to the left) and knock his butt or blade to the side with your bayonet or rifle stock. See Figure 98.

2. Come up and into him with a hard butt stroke to his crotch.

The squat parry is used purely in defensive situations such as might occur if you tripped and fell while fighting. You can Squat Parry from either knee and even from your back or side, although with more difficulty. (Demonstrate all of these possibilities.) The squat parry can also be executed from a whirl to meet a sudden attack from the rear. If you see the attacker very close behind you, execute a whirl but instead of coming to "on guard" as you face to the rear, drop to your right knee planting your rifle butt on the deck, and execute a squat parry on his thrust or buttstroke. Follow through with a vertical buttstroke to the crotch. (Demonstrate a couple times.)

(5) The Squat Parry can also be used in case you have more than one man after you with the bayonet and are backing away. When one pursuing enemy is about to thrust you, suddenly drop into the squat guard position and execute a squat parry and follow through. (Demonstrate.) Don't worry about what you do with the other enemy in the meantime. You'll learn that next hour.

(6) (Instructor's Note). — The instructor then forms the unit in four ranks for "contact" work with the square guard and parry and the squat guard and parry. He conducts the men through the practice at first "by the numbers" so that they can experience how the parries are made. Then the exercise is conducted without the numbers but controlled by initial commands. Both ranks start at the On Guard position before each move commences.

(7) For the Square Guard practice, the commands will be "Inboard Ranks, Long Thrust; Outboard Ranks; Square Guard and Parry; 1. Stand By, 2. MOVE." The square guard may also be practiced against buttstrokes. Simulated follow-throughs by the men executing the square parry will aways be carried out.

The instructor will conduct the square guard and parry practice in this manner perhaps ten times and then will give the men the valuable experience of having the attack that they counter come from the side. To accomplish this the instructor will initially have the ranks who are to make the counter, face either left, half left, right or half right. Then the exercise is continued as before. The men making the square parry will pivot away from and face to the direction of the attack as they come to square guard and make the parry. This practice will continue for about a dozen or so moves.

(8) For the Squat Guard practice the commands will be: "Inboard Ranks, Long Thrust; Outboard Ranks, Squat Guard and Parry; 1. Stand by, 2. MOVE." When the men are proficient at this, then the squat guard is combined with a whirl to counter the attack from the rear. All ranks are first faced in the same direction. Then the commands are: "Inboard Ranks, Long Thrust; Outboard Ranks, Whirl and Squat Parry; 1. Stand By, 2. MOVE." The parry will also be practiced against the buttstrokes.

(9) If more than fifteen minutes still remains, then contact work with the newly learned feints, Gain-Point-High-Slash-Low and Gain-Point-Low-Slash-High, will be in

order. The same initial "Four Ranks" formation will be employed. For about the first dozen times one rank will "stand fast" while the other rank executes the feint the instructor designates by his command: "Inboard Ranks, Stand Fast; Outboard Ranks, Gain-Point-High-Slash-Low. 1. Stand By, 2. MOVE." The men "standing fast" will be told not to try to outguess the man making the feint but to react as they would involuntarily if the feint really were a surprise to them. Then the men will be given an opportunity to see how good their feints actually have become. The instructor will tell the men that the rank making the feint can use either feint that they wish and those standing fast can try to outguess the aggressors and block their moves. The instructor's command will be: "Inboard Ranks, Stand Fast; Outboard Ranks, Gain-and-Point; 1. Stand by, 2. MOVE." This practice will continue for about a dozen times, alternating the inboard and outboard ranks as the aggressors.

(10) If there is still more than fifteen minutes left, the men will stay in the same relative position and will practice feints and parries uncontrolled but supervised closely by company instructors.

(11) Both halves of the company will then run the entire bayonet course, finishing up the hour. Each man will go through the course twice, the first time medium speed and the second time fast.

33. 17th Hour of Combat Conditioning.—(Instructor's Note.) Thirty (30) minutes before the hour begins five (5) company NCOs will be rehearsed in a demonstration of Group Assault Tactics by one of the Combat Conditioning Section instructors. At the scheduled time, the Company will be assembled with surveyed rifles, short bayonets, and scabbards fixed.

a. **Review.**—The Combat Conditioning Section instructor will review all bayonet work to date and other CC instructors will demonstrate. He will take these movements in sequence, describing each one rapidly and, in addition, **emphasizing** the following:

(1) **Grip.**—Entirely natural, allowing a firm hold without unnecessary straining. Avoid an "on edge" or "flat grip". Forearm along comb of stock is optional—good for thrusts. Butt not against right hip.

(2) **Stance.**—Weight poised on balls of feet, comfortably apart and left somewhat advanced. Knees slightly bent, body bent slightly forward. Bayonet always pointing towards base of opponent's throat. Keep your eyes on your opponent and his blade. If practicing alone, keep eyes on tip of your own bayonet.

(3) **Foot-work**—(as demonstrated by foot-drill).—Light, quick shuffle. Never cross feet except on "Front-Pass" or "Rear-Pass".

(4)   **Hurdling & Vaulting.**—Don't change grip.

(5)   **Long Thrust.**—Use forearm for support on stock, guide thrust with left hand. Bend right knee and reach way out. Straighten arms at last second of lunge. **Do not wave the point.** Make it travel straight—your bayonet, rifle, and all moving in a line coinciding with their own long axes. Put your whole body into it. **Withdraw** automatically with a hard jerk back along the line of penetration.

(6)   **Short Thrust.**—Same as long thrust, except left foot advanced. Make it vigorous and fast. Strive for accuracy.

(7)   **Buttstrokes and Slashes.**—Ordinarily used when opponent is inside your blade. The movements must come rapidly, instinctively, and aggressively. Strike instantly for any opening that appears. Don't let up until your enemy is destroyed. The buttstroke sequence emphasizes aggression.

(8)   **Straight Parries.**—Combined with a thrust—a hard deflection blow to his blade, delivered by your blade by moving your rifle sharply, laterally a short distance. Use vigorous wrist and arm motion in the parry and the ensuing thrust.

(9)   **Hand & Arm Signals—Pairs.**—Emphasize speed, coordination, and reaction. Also the necessity for being close at the start of each movement and pulling no punches.

(10)   **Shift Parries.**—Effective way of getting inside of an opponent's blade for a quick kill. Can be used aggressively or counteroffensively. Must keep your eyes on enemy's blade and shift your body laterally before contacting his blade.

(11)   **Reverse & Change Over.**—Primarily for developing skill in manipulation of rifle and bayonet. Not emphasized for combat use as such.

(12)   **Feints.**—Of secondary importance but can be quite valuable in the attack. Must be done rapidly and followed up without hesitation. May be supplemented by parries while working into an enemy.

(13)   **Square Guard Parries and Squat Parries.**—Good in sudden defensive situations where you have neither the room nor the time to counter in another way.

(14)   The instructor answers any questions that occur. Then the candidates will turn to in platoon areas working on each other and reviewing all bayonet movements to date except foot-drill, hurdling and vaulting, hand signals, and reverse, and change over. Instructors will check up and insure that all scabbards are fixed and are safe and sound at all times. (10 minutes).

(15)   Troops will then run through the bayonet course twice. Instructors will be stationed at each target, and will keep the troops moving, making necessary corrections and promoting the spirit of aggressiveness in the men. Then they will assemble for work on simple group assault tactics.

b. **Group Assault Tactics.**—(1) G e n e r a l.—The instructor: While actual bayonet fighting is individual, each man must understand from the very first that he is fighting for his organization and not for himself alone. When one body of Marines assaults the position of another group, none can know which enemy he will engage until the attackers get within bayonet range. No man knows whether he will be suddenly confronted and attacked by several enemies at the same time, or if one of several friends will confront a single enemy. The fighters who have the teamwork, skill, and presence of mind to capitalize quickly on such inequalities will gain momentary numerical advantage. It must be borne in mind that the bayonet fight is generally but of a few seconds duration and that the action must be fast to be successful.

If two Marines, suddenly confronting one of the enemy, are able to put him out of action in a few seconds, they can quickly turn on another opponent. Such systematic assaults occurring in the first critical seconds of meeting in hand-to-hand fighting may reduce the enemy's initial strength by many men. In another few seconds these tactics can operate with annihilating effect on the remainder of the enemy. However, if assault groups lack a prearranged system of team attack, a single enemy can hold off a pair of bayonet fighters for a few seconds, by which time one of his comrades may rush to his assistance and end the two-to-one advantage which existed.

To be effective, group assault tactics must be **simple** and **flexible,** since it is impossible to predict what the exact situation will be until the opposing fighters are within a few paces of each other. Movements are fast and automatic, for the quickness and turmoil of hand-to-hand fighting will rarely permit verbal coordination of attack.

(2) **Two against One.**—1. **Approach.**—Two bayonet fighters, part of an assaulting echelon approach a single enemy. Since these fighters cannot know what the opponent will do, they cannot plan for coordinated action at this stage. Hence, they advance directly forward on a run, **neither one converging on the opponent.**

2. **Contact.**—As the fighters get within bayonet range, one of them initially will be opposed by the single enemy. The selected man advances upon him in a frontal attack. The other man quickly advances until opposite the opponent's flank and then turns sharply to strike his exposed flank or rear. See Figure 98a, b, c, d.

R.D. 4443

Figure 98(a).—Group Assault Tactics; 2 vs. 1—Part 1.

Figure 98(b).—Group Assault Tactics; 2 vs. 1—Part 2.

Figure 98(c).—Group Assault Tactics; 2 vs. 1—Part 3.

Figure 98(d).—Group Assault Tactics; 2 vs. 1—Part 4.

3. **Alternative Attack.**—If the enemy turns suddenly toward the flanking fighter to fend him off, he thereby exposes himself to the fighter making the frontal attack. This man strikes instantly. In any such coordinated attack, the man who makes the kill usually is the one who is not closely engaged with the enemy's bayonet. The entire operation is carried out in a few seconds. The approach, contact, and attack flow into one continuous assault. (Demonstration by Company NCO Instructors.)

(3) **One Against Two.**—Where two of the enemy confront one Marine, this man darts forward and immediately turns to the flank of one or the other enemy. **Under no circumstances does he permit himself to be caught between them.** By moving quickly to one side or the other, whichever is more expedient, he keeps the nearer enemy between himself and the farther enemy, and concentrates on disposing of one enemy at a time. See Figures 99a; b, c, d, e, f. (Demonstration by Company NCO instructors.)

R.D. 4443

Figure 99(a).—Group Assault Tactics; 1 vs. 2—Part 1.

Figure 99(b).—Group Assault Tactics: 1 vs. 2—Part 2.

Figure 99(c).—Group Assault Tactics; 1 vs. 2—Part 3.

R.D. 4443

Figure 99(d).—Group Assault Tactics; 1 vs. 2—Part 4.

R.D. 4443

Figure 99(e).—Group Assault Tactics; 1 vs. 2—Part 5.

R.D. 4443

Figure 99(f).—Group Assault Tactics; 1 vs. 2—Part 6.

(4) **Three Against Two.**—1. **Approach.**—Three attackers approach two of the enemy. At this stage none of the three knows who will be engaged initially by the enemy. They advance directly forward at a run.

2. **Contact.**—As they get within bayonet range, two of the attackers will normally be engaged by two of the enemy. One attacker is thus left momentarily free. He continues directly forward until opposite the flank of the nearest or most accessible enemy, at which exposed side, as in the two-against-one maneuver. The other two attackers maintain their frontal attacks. With one enemy disposed of, the other enemy is struck in the flank by the first free attacker

275

who can reach him. If either enemy being attacked on his flank turns to defend himself, he leaves himself open to the attacker making the frontal assault. (Demonstration by Company NCO Instructors.)

(5) **Two Against Three.**—In a situation where two bayonet fighters are confronted by three of the enemy, they dart to the flanks, leaving the enemy in the center the last to be encountered. When one of the attackers has disposed of his opponent, he immediately attacks the remaining enemy. (Demonstration by Company NCO Instructors.)

(6) (Instructor's Note). — **Practice.**—Candidates then turn to in platoon areas under supervision of platoon instructors and practice group assault tactics: first two against one, then one vs. two; next three vs. two, then two vs. three. Instructors will see that all bayonet scabbards are in good condition and fixed at all times; that opposing sides are dressed distinctively (i.e., one side with shirts or caps and the other without); that there is no undue fencing around. All thrusts and slashes should stop just short of the mark or barely make contact. Buttstrokes will be "pulled" and must not land. Candidates should be able to apply all the bayonet fighting technique they have learned. Instructors must constantly stress aggressiveness within the limits of the personal safety of the candidates. Finish up the hour with group assault tactics. Instructors should decide which candidates should represent their respective platoons in the competition at the beginning of the next hour.

34. 18th Hour of Combat Conditioning; 8th Hour of Bayonet.—(Notes for Instructors).

a. **Group Assault Competition.**—Company assembled in a large semi-circle for inter-platoon bayonet competition. Each platoon will have three to five men selected by the platoon's, instructors to represent the platoon. Two or more bouts will be scheduled, depending upon how much time is available. The bouts might run something like this:

(1) 1 man, 1st Plat. vs. 2 men, 2d Plat.
(2) 2 men, 1st Plat. vs. 3 men, 3d Plat.

If there is more time available then more bouts involving unequal sides can be worked in. All company instructors will be scattered along the inner edge of the semi-circle where they can best see the action. They will all act as judges for the bouts. The opposing sides for any bout will line up facing each other in the space provided about ten yards apart. For a side having more than one man there will be a 5-pace interval between men. Each man will have a sound scabbard affixed firmly to his bayonet. All scabbards will be inspected before the action starts. For purposes of identification the men representing each platoon will dress distinctively—say, for example, no cap or no jacket or something else missing. All scabbards may be dipped into powdered lime to help determine a hit being scored with the bayonet. The sides will move out from this position on "MOVE". The judges must watch the action carefully to see when a vital spot is "hit". They must see that the scabbards stay on the bayonets and that there is no unnecessary roughness. (The purpose of the competition is merely to add interest to bayonet technique and group assault tactics.)

Save the last half hour for work in bayonet and rifle disarming. The company assembles in the sawdust square for a few words about bayonet training and then a demonstration of disarming techniques.

b. **Bayonet Training for Marines—Recapitulation of the Bayonet Program.**—(1) Now that the bayonet training course is over here, we might spend a minute or two discussing the program. Before we got under way at all we tried to explain why we were having you men out here during bayonet work at all. You all knew that most Marine Infantry troops carry the bayonet as a secondary weapon. You weren't sure just why much emphasis was placed upon bayonet training at recruit camp, at New River or San Diego or here at Officer Candidates School—especially those of you who had seen action or been in touch with Japanese, because you knew that shells, grenades, and bullets most often did the dirty work. Well, now that you men are about to become officers and have seen something of bayonet training you should know, if you don't already, what we hope to accomplish by a bayonet training program.

(2) Bayonet Training has a three-fold purpose. **The first of these is to promote the spirit of aggressiveness.** This is accomplished by practice of basic thrusts, buttstrokes and parries in aggressive fighting sequences. Essential to their application are bayonet and assault courses where the men get the idea of attacking and pressing on incessantly. This is important in the actual assault, where you will get out of your cover and charge in with your heart in your mouth, but, nevertheless, not without a certain sense of automatic response to your leader's signal or command. Actual contact work in practice increases your confidence, too.

(3) The second purpose is **physical condition**. Marines must have stamina and physical strength in order to train and to fight at all effectively day after day. They get this to quite an extent from vigorous bayonet training and assault courses. Of course field work is essential in this respect too.

(4) The third purpose is all around **bayonet fighting ability.** This is probably much more important in the way that it affects and bolsters the confidence of the individual Marine in himself as a fighting man, than it is in its actual application on the battlefield. If a man has learned to use the

bayonet aggressively and to a lesser extent defensively, he will not hesitate to close with the enemy whether it will be with flying bullets or with cold steel. And when he should meet the enemy, bayonet against bayonet, he has a good chance of coming out the victor.

c. **Bayonet System for Marines.**—(1)   We don't have much time to spend on bayonet work in any part of the training of the Marine. There are too many other important things that require the time and energy available. If we did have the time, we could spend more of it on the individual as we do in rifle marksmanship and really turn out a snappy product. But we don't, and consequently, must have a bayonet training program which will accomplish the three purposes of bayonet training in the order of priority and in a relatively short period of time.

(2)   The first thing that must be taught a Marine and stressed throughout his training is the fundamentals: grip, stance, footwork, thrusts, buttstrokes, straight parries, and fighting sequences. He learns how to roll and jump with the bayonet. With these simple moves mastered, a Marine has acquired aggressiveness and confidence. He also has a fairly good chance against the average Jap bayonet fighter. He will be in fairly good physical shape from the bayonet drill and assault courses. The fundamentals are readily taught to fairly large-sized groups of men by a limited group of instructors—a point which must be borne in mind.

(3)   Add to the Marine's repertoire a few simple and effective additional parries and a basic feint or two and you will have increased his abilities and potentialities as a bayonet fighter. He will also have greater confidence in himself. Moreover these new moves are not very hard to teach to medium-sized groups of Marines, provided all the instructors know and can teach the moves readily. Despite their undenied effectiveness these moves are more complicated than the fundamental thrusts, parries, and buttstrokes already taught. Therefore they are taught only after the fundamentals have been mastered. Group assault fighting tactics are then included.

(4)   There are further simple refinements involving moves (such as feints and parries) which are applied only in certain cases. These are left until last and are taught only after the first basic moves and techniques have been mastered. Unless they are practiced for some time they will be forgotten and never used in the excitement of the assault.

(5)   Throughout the program one system of grip, stance, and footwork has been stressed from which all the movements taught can be used readily. You have had but eight hours here. A regular course for enlisted men (and for you also for that matter) covering the same material might well last for two or three times that much. It would simply involve more of the same work you have had and in addition

would entail more competition throughout and also assault course running and body-strengthening exercises. They would be some bare-blade contact work too.

    d. **Rifle and Bayonet Disarming.**

    (Note for Instructors.)

    (This may well be introduced after Pistol Disarming is covered in the 8th training hour. It could then be reviewed and practiced, during this last hour of training.

    (1) **General.**—The CC Section Instructor: Rifle and bayonet disarming is perhaps more important for Marines to know than any other type of disarming because the need for its use is more apt to occur. This is simply because the enemy uses more rifles and bayonets than they do other personal weapons. You might have the misfortune to lose your rifle or to have it broken in a melee of some sort. The first thing that you would do, of course, would be to try and get any weapon as soon as possible and continue to fight. But in the meantime you might be attacked by an enemy armed with rifle and bayonet in which case you must react just as aggressively as if you too were armed. Get set for a close-in attack and time it for the instant that your opponent has charged or committed himself to a thrust from which he is unable to recover to counter your own sudden maneuver. Take away his weapon from him and kill him with it.

    The basic principles you must remember for disarming are:

    1. Don't "telegraph" or give away your move to your attacker before he charges.

    2. Whatever move you make, make it at the last possible moment and at top speed—otherwise he will counter it easily.

    3. Wherever possible expedite your diarming moves by suddenly throwing anything available into his eyes and kneeing or kicking him in any vital spot.

    Naturally, effective bayonet disarming ability requires a good deal of practice—more than we have time to devote to it. We will teach you only two disarming moves. These will take care of just about any situation that you'll run up against. One of them is especially good if the attacker rushes you; the other is good if the attacker comes in more slowly.

    (2) **Parry Left, Over-the-Shoulder**—the best if attacker comes at you slow or medium speed.

    1. Twist your body to the left and back from the hips, pivoting on the ball of your right foot, and parry the bayonet to the left with the palm of your right hand against the side of the blade. See Figure 100a.

Figure 100(a).—**Bayonet Disarming**—Parry Left—Over Shoulder—
Part 1.

Figure 100(b).—Bayonet Disarming—Parry Left—Over Shoulder—
Part 2.

2. Step forward to his left side with your left foot and as you do, come up hard underneath the front hand guard with the palm of your left hand, grasp it, and force the rifle up and backward in an arc toward his shoulder.

3. Quickly come down hard with the cutting edge of your right hand inside his left elbow, thus helping to break his hold with his left hand on the rifle. Pull back on his upper forearm towards you with your right hand. See Figure 100b.

4. Move past his left side. Jerk the rifle up and in an arc over his shoulder increasing your leverage by grabbing hold with your right hand above your left on the front hand guard and forcing the rifle back and over. If he is strong, expedite the break by kicking his knees and legs with your left heel. Use your left forearm to get leverage. See Figure 100c.

Figure 100(c).—Bayonet Disarming—Parry Left—Over Shoulder— Part 3.

Figure 100(d).—Bayonet Disarming—Parry Left—Over Shoulder—Part 4.

5. When you have wrenched the rifle free retain your original grip with your left hand,—Figure 100d—catch the small of the stock with your right hand as you whirl to face your enemy. Kill him with the bayonet and rifle.

This disarming move sounds complicated—but it is not tricky and can be learned quite easily. It is a safe method to use because you do not depend too much on his momentum to help you and his reactions need not bother you too much.

(3) **Deck Parry—Right.**—Best used when opponent rushes you with the bayonet.

1. Step back to the left rear with your right foot, pivoting on the ball of your left foot, thus getting out of the way of the blade.

2. With the palm of your right hand knock his bayonet blade or better yet his front guard down to the deck. Retain a grasp on the front hand guard. If you hit it hard enough and if he is coming fast, his blade may stick in the deck and he'll pile up on his rifle.

3. Step to your left with your left foot, quickly grab the toe of his butt with your left hand, get your shoulder behind it and push to the right (his original front). This will wrench the rifle from his grasp.

4. Change hands on the rifle (Reverse) and attack him with it and the bayonet.

When worked fast, this disarming move will throw the attacker forward onto the deck. It should not be used if the thrust is not fast and vigorous, because it would be fairly easy for the attacker to buttstroke you.

(4) **Disarming From the Rear.**—If you are being taken a prisoner from behind or marched along by an enemy armed with a rifle and bayonet who is pressing the bayonet tip against your back, you have a chance to disarm him. Naturally you should wait until you think that he is sufficiently off guard before you go into action. You may or may not have your hands raised. You can work it either way.

1. Whirl your body (from the hips) around to the left knocking the bayonet to the right with your left elbow and arm as you do and getting your body out of the line of fire in case you should miss the parry. See Figures 101a, b.

Figure 101(a).—Bayonet Disarming from Rear—Part 1.

Figure 101(b).—Bayonet Disarming from Rear—Part 2.

2. Step up to his left side and work the Over-the-Shoulder Disarming Move.

(Demonstrate twice fast.)

Notice that you whirl to the left—not the right. Should you whirl to the right you will be all set to catch a butt-stroke. (Demonstrate.) See Figure 101c.

R.D. 4443

Figure 101(c).—Bayonet Disarming from Rear—Part 3.

(5) **Defense for a Fallen, Unarmed Marine Against a Bayonet Attack.**—This is a very undesirable, yet entirely conceivable situation. Speed and surprise are required to make the defense succeed. From your position on your back,

hook one toe behind the ankle of your enemy's leading foot and pull, and with your other foot kick his knee-cap or shin just below the knee as hard as you can. This will set him down to the deck in a hurry if properly done.

(6) Leading a Prisoner.

Figure 102.—Leading a Prisoner.

If you should be taking an enemy prisoner or marching him along, keep him ahead of you and five or six feet away from the bayonet so he can't surprise you and grab the rifle. If he should need prodding then either scare him with a few threatening moves or come to high port or short guard and kick him in the back. See Figure 102.

Pair off and turn to in platoon areas, practicing disarming for the rest of the hour.

(7) **Japanese Bayonet Technique.**—If time still permits CC Section instructors give a brief demonstration of Japanese bayonet technique.

35. Bayonet and Assault Courses.

(Instructor's Notes.)

a. **Bayonet Course.**—On the following pages are shown diagrams and an outline of the four-lane Bayonet Course used at the Officer Candidates School. They are self-explanatory. See Figures 103, 103a, 103b, and 103c.

(1)   The bayonet course utilized a previously constructed old style bayonet course, with simple parry sticks, thrust dummies, and buttstroke and jab targets. Some of these targets were modified and a few additional targets and obstacles were added to fit in with the current bayonet training methods. The alterations consisted of fixing some of the parry sticks so that they could be parried down as well as to one side. This was a very simple operation which involved minor carpentering work with the parry stick and its pivot and the installation of a few more door springs. The additions to the old course consisted of digging standing type foxholes at the start, and a couple of shallow ditches (one filled with sawdust) and of building a four-foot fence; a low trip rail at the head of the sawdust-filled ditch, and swinging smash and slash dummies. The old posts with portions of rubber tire affixed throat-high, which had previously been used for the new obsolete "jab", were moved back from the thrust dummy that they followed and became used as single targets to feint and thrust or slash at.

(2)   The purposes of the bayonet course are: to let the men practice the bayonet techniques under "running" conditions, to let them work up some endurance, to bolster their individual aggressive spirits, and to let them see how a bayonet course might be laid out and constructed.

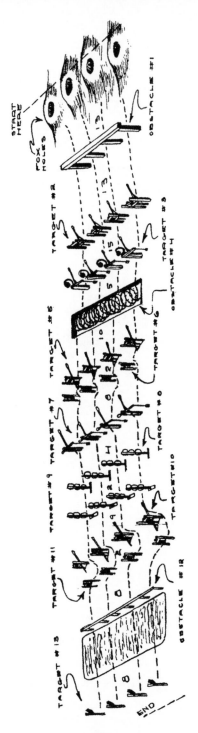

START HERE

FOX HOLES

OBSTACLE #1

TARGET #2

TARGET #3

OBSTACLE #4

TARGET #5

TARGET #7

TARGET #9

TARGET #11

TARGET #13

OBSTACLE #6

TARGET #8

TARGET #10

OBSTACLE #12

END

289

Number of Obst. or Targ.	Dist., Yd., between Fronts of—	Plan of Course
	13	3 @ 10 = 30'
1	13	30'
2	15	30'
3	5	30'
4	10	30' Width of Course is 30' Throughout

RD 4443

Target Detail	Description, Action Requ'd.
	Standing Type, Foxhole. Start from within with fixed bayonet.
4'	Log Rail. Vault over using one hand to assist. Don't change grip on rifle.
	Standard Brush Dummy with Parry Stick. Straight Parry Right and Long Thrust.
	Standard Swinging Bag with Parry Stick. Straight Parry Left and Horizontal Butt Stroke.
8' Concertina Barbed Wire	Shallow Ditch w/concertina wire. Hurdle, throwing rifle overhead and bringing it down on landing.

Number of Obst. or Targ.	Dist., Yd., between Fronts of—	Plan of Course
5	2	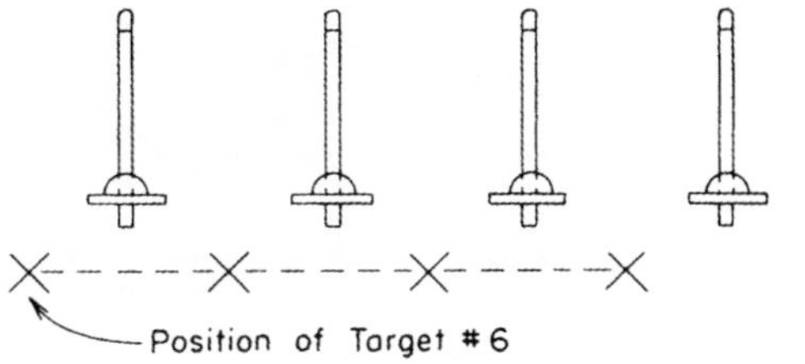 Position of Target # 6
6	8	
7	4	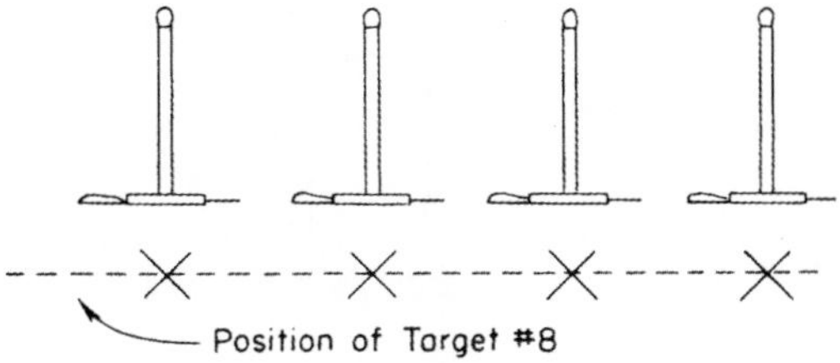 Position of Target #8
8	2.	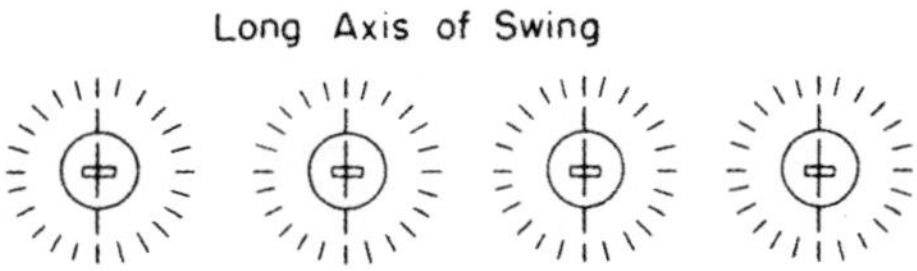 Long Axis of Swing
9	9	

RD 4443

293

Target Detail	Description, Action Requ'd.
	Modified Standard Brush Dummy with Parry Stick. Shift Parry Left, and Slash or Thrust.
	Standard Thrust Dummy. Brush. Short Thrust.
	Standard Vertical Butt Stroke Dummy with modified Parry Stick. Shift Parry Left and Vertical Butt Stroke.

	Swinging Butt and Slash Dummies with targets for head, throat, and crotch.
	
	Springs and platform countersunk.
	   Target #8—Smash.
	   Target #9—Slash.

Number of Obst. or Targ.	Dist., Yd., between Fronts of—	Plan of Course
10	2	
11	4	
12	8	
13		

RD 4443

Target Detail	Description, Action Req'd.
Modified Thrust Dummy—Same as #5. Thrust Dummy—Same as #6.	Shift Parry Right and Thrust or Slash Throat. Short Thrust.
Sawdust 1'	Low Rail and shallow Sawdust Pit. Dive over rail and roll with rifle in pit.
5'	Feint targets: rubber tire on wooden post tops. Feint at target, then quickly slash or thrust. Finish course by simulating two quick aimed or hip shots.

b. **Combat Conditioning Course.**—Four Lanes—Run by Four-man Teams.

(1)   On the following pages are shown self-explanatory diagrams—Figures 104, 104a-104e inclusive—and photographs—Figures 105-118 inclusive—of the Combat Conditioning Course used by men of the Officer Candidates School. It is shown here as a suggested guide for similar courses for use in various units of the Marine Corps. Naturally, the construction and types of obstacles in any such course will depend in great part on the materials available.

(2)   The course at Officer Candidates School was designed to give the men an all-around physical workout and also to give them practice in working together in the assault. The course starts off with work mainly with the arms, hands, and shoulders where the men scale a wall, swing across the pit by rope and traverse elevated, horizontal logs, hand-over-hand. This covers a distance of about 60 yards. The men then run through about 240 yards of various assault obstacles, using the bayonet freely and hitting the deck frequently. The total distance covered is about 300 yards, plenty for building up endurance if run through regularly. In addition to the physical workout aspect of the course, the Officer Candidates are given a chance to study the layout of the course and acquaint themselves with materials used and method of construction.

(3)   The course is located in a fairly low area and horseshoes around a small creek. The first half of the course is in fairly open woods; the second half is just outside the woods and runs through considerable scrub growth. All scrub growth and trees, except those that constituted a potential bodily menace to the candidates running through the course, were left standing, thus leaving the visibility as poor as possible and requiring the men to sharpen their eyesight and reactions as well as to get used to moving through brush on the double. Obstacles were constructed of natural materials where possible. The only artificial materials used were ropes, barbed and smooth wire, and spikes. The time for a single man running the course (after some practice) at top speed is about three to three and a half minutes. For four-men teams running through a good time would be five or six minutes.

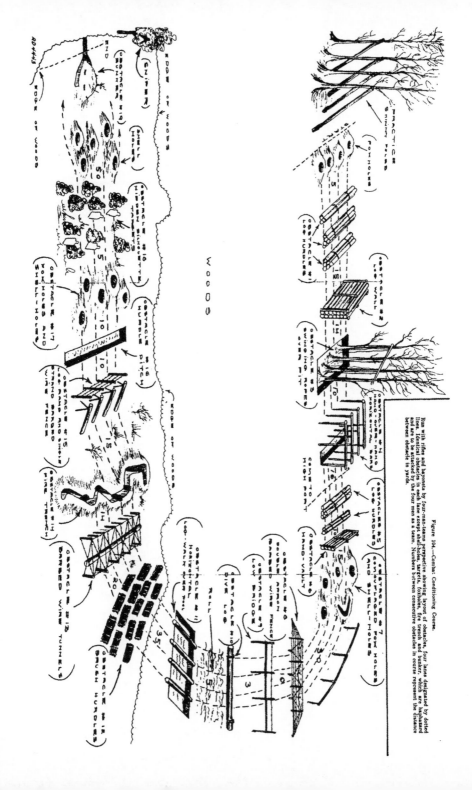

Figure 104.—Combat Conditioning Course.

Run with rifles and bayonets by four-man-teams perspective showing layout of obstacles, four lanes designated by dotted lines. Identical obstacles in each lane except shell-holes, foxholes, fire trench and bunker, which are haphazard and are to be attacked by the four men as a team. Numbers between consecutive obstacles in course represent the distance between obstacle in yards.

No. of Obst.	Dist., Yd. Between Fronts of Obstacles	Plan of Course
	7	← 3 @ 10 = 30' →
	5	← 3 @ 10 = 30' →
1	15	← 30' →
2	14	← 30' →

RD 4443

Obstacle Detail	Description and Action Required
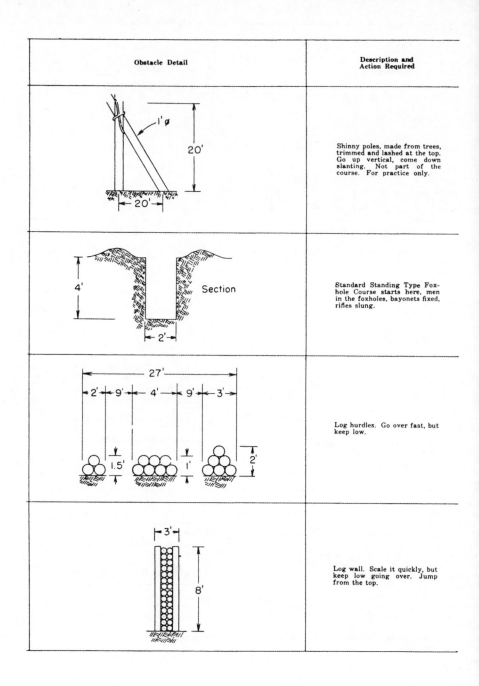	Shinny poles, made from trees, trimmed and lashed at the top. Go up vertical, come down slanting. Not part of the course. For practice only.
	Standard Standing Type Foxhole Course starts here, men in the foxholes, bayonets fixed, rifles slung.
	Log hurdles. Go over fast, but keep low.
	Log wall. Scale it quickly, but keep low going over. Jump from the top.

No. of Obst.	Dist., Yd. Between Fronts of Obstacles	Plan of Course
3	10	Four $1\frac{1}{4}$" - 50' Ropes
4	16	3 @ 8 = 24'
		UNSLING RIFLE ANI
5	10	Same as Obstacle #1
6	15	
7	30	

RD 4443

Obstacle Detail	Description and Action Required
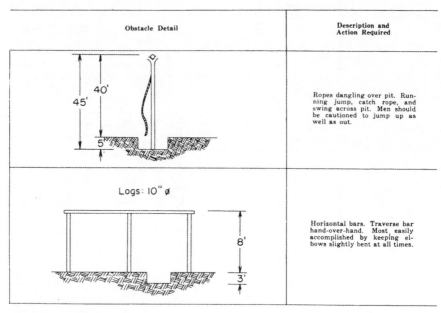	Ropes dangling over pit. Running jump, catch rope, and swing across pit. Men should be cautioned to jump up as well as out.
	Horizontal bars. Traverse bar hand-over-hand. Most easily accomplished by keeping elbows slightly bent at all times.

GET UP TO HIGH PORT

Same as Obstacle #1	Log Hurdles.
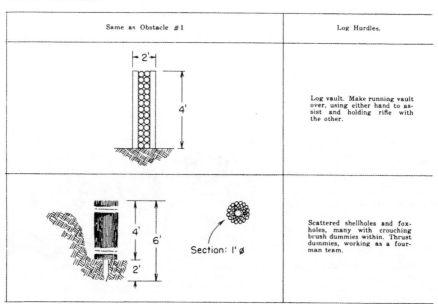	Log vault. Make running vault over, using either hand to assist and holding rifle with the other.
	Scattered shellholes and foxholes, many with crouching brush dummies within. Thrust dummies, working as a four-man team.

No. of Obst.	Dist., Yd. Between Fronts of Obstacles	Plan of Course
8	10	
9	3	
10	5	
11	35	

RD 4443

Obstacle Detail	Description and Action Required
	Standard Double Apron Barbed Wire Fence. Crawn under using proper technique.
	Low bridge (single B. W. strand and rail). Run underneath, keeping low.
Log: 1' ⌀ Smoothed Ground 15'	Log trip and rolling area. Dive over the log and roll correctly with the rifle, ending up on your feet and "on guard."
Log: 1' ⌀ 4'	Horizontal logs laid across water pool. Cross over on logs quickly.

No. of Obst.	Dist., Yd. Between Fronts of Obstacles	Plan of Course
12	20	
13	14	
14	15	
15	10	

RD 4443

Obstacle Detail	Description and Action Required
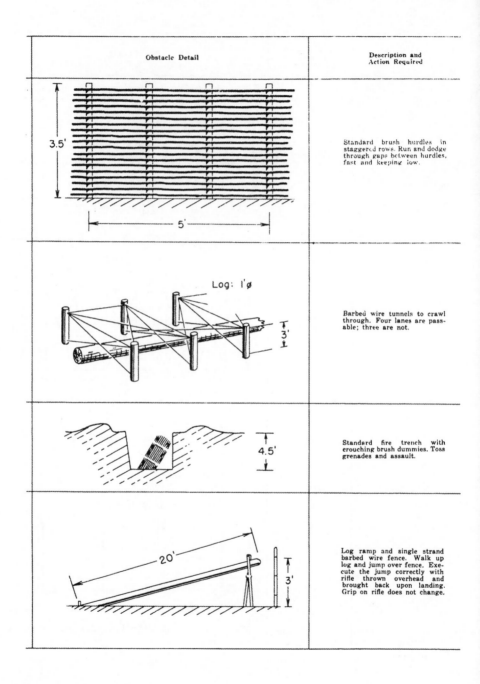	Standard brush hurdles in staggered rows. Run and dodge through gaps between hurdles, fast and keeping low.
	Barbed wire tunnels to crawl through. Four lanes are passable; three are not.
	Standard fire trench with crouching brush dummies. Toss grenades and assault.
	Log ramp and single strand barbed wire fence. Walk up log and jump over fence. Execute the jump correctly with rifle thrown overhead and brought back upon landing. Grip on rifle does not change.

No. of Obst.	Dist., Yd. Between Fronts of Obstacles	Plan of Course
16	10	30'
17	5	
18	15	
19	50	

RD 4443

Obstacle Detail	Description and Action Required
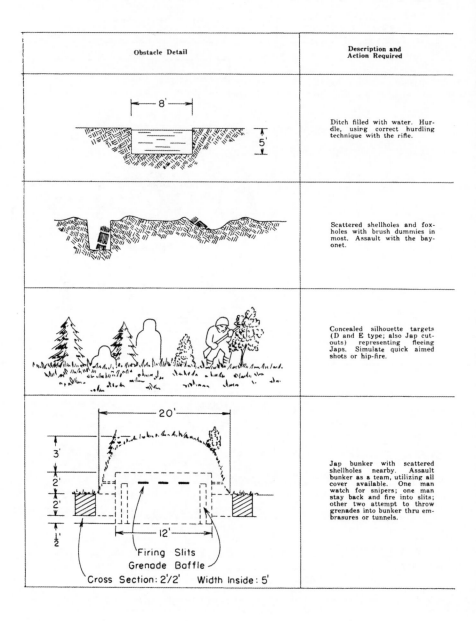	Ditch filled with water. Hurdle, using correct hurdling technique with the rifle.
	Scattered shellholes and foxholes with brush dummies in most. Assault with the bayonet.
	Concealed silhouette targets (D and E type; also Jap cutouts) representing fleeing Japs. Simulate quick aimed shots or hip-fire.
	Jap bunker with scattered shellholes nearby. Assault bunker as a team, utilizing all cover available. One man watch for snipers; one man stay back and fire into slits; other two attempt to throw grenades into bunker thru embrasures or tunnels.

Figure 105.—Combat Conditioning Course, Obstacle #2.

Figure 106.—Combat Conditioning Course, Obstacle #3.

Figure 107.—Combat Conditioning Course, Obstacle #4.

Figure 108.—Combat Conditioning Course, Obstacle #6.

Figure 109.—Combat Conditioning Course, Obstacle #7.

Figure 110.—Combat Conditioning Course, Obstacle #8.

Figure 111.—Combat Conditioning Course, Obstacle #9, 10.

317

Figure 112.—Combat Conditioning Course, Obstacle #11.

Figure 113.—Combat Conditioning Course, Obstacle #12.

Figure 114.—Combat Conditioning Course, Obstacle #13.

Figure 115.—Combat Conditioning Course, Obstacle #14.

Figure 116.—Combat Conditioning Course, Obstacle #15.

Figure 117.—Combat Conditioning Course, Obstacle #16.

323

Figure 118.—Combat Conditioning Course, Obstacle #17, 18.

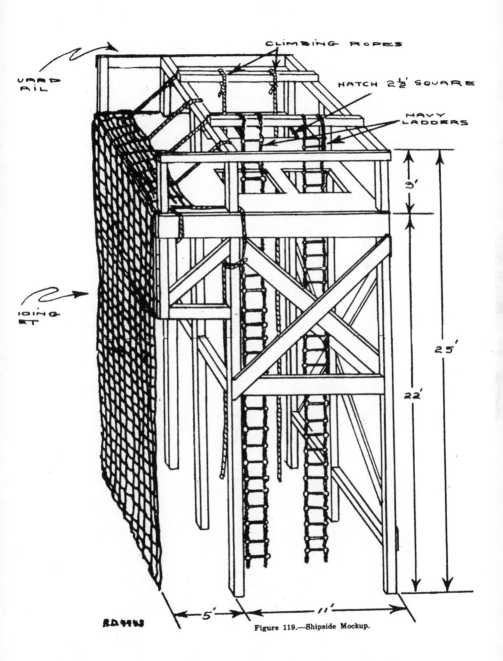

CLIMBING ROPES

HATCH 2½' SQUARE

NAVY LADDERS

GUARD RAIL

3'

25'

22'

LOADING NET

5'

11'

R.D.H.W.

Figure 119.—Shipside Mockup.

INDEX